GATHERER
OF SOULS

Lorna Smithers

GATHERER OF SOULS

Lorna Smithers

ISBN: 978-1-7357944-5-7

Gods&Radicals Press
an imprint of RITONA a.s.b.l
3 Rue de Wormeldange
Rodenbourg, Luxembourg
L-1695

Layout and Design: Rhyd Wildermuth
Cover Image: Tom Brown (hoplelessmaine.com)

View our catalogue and online journal at
ABEAUTIFULRESISTANCE.ORG

For the dead,
the mad,
and the poets.
Foremost for
Gwyn ap Nudd.

'For beauty is nothing but the beginning of terror
which we are barely able to endure, and it amazes us so,
because it serenely disdains to destroy us'
Rainer Maria Rilke

'To know a god you must go mad'
Rhyd Wildermuth

'Gwyn is not only a guide into Annwn but also mysteriously
connected with the end of a world... Gwyn may be seen
as a guide into the next human world'
Nicolas R. Mann

Contents

Between Sky and Air—114

VI The Brink of Time—133

Acknowledgements—154

Missing God

I knew you were there from the day I was born
because I needed you.

I could not find your name in the Bible
or scrawled on church walls,

there was something about the Devil,
but no...

The feeling in my navel kept tugging me
through the portals in the books I read about sundered
worlds.

They opened something and I fell into you
but I didn't know what you were,

(that a god could be the underworld).

I searched the absences
and filled my hands with empty air

and filled my ears with words without sound.
I danced and raised my hands to the sky

but only found you when I fell to the ground.
I drank my way back to you living

in the epoché where the rules of Thisworld
fall away like empty shells

and all the hidden people are revealed,
the times piled on top of one another like broken cars.

You showed me silver spaceships,
three shining gateways,

pathways to the stars that always led back down.
Your world - you - were so beautiful you frightened me.

I returned to my shell
but could not deny what you are or what I am.

Eventually you showed me your face and told me your
 name.

Gatherer of Souls

'Not made of air at all, but of ghost – the substance of quintillions of quintillions of generations of souls blended into one immense translucency – souls of people who thought in ways never resembling our ways'
  Lafcadio Hearn

I met him on the tear-drenched edgelands between madness and reason, dreaming and waking, life and death. Gwyn ap Nudd opened the doors of Annwn and called me to ride with him into the mists through the war-torn centuries to recover his forgotten mythos.

On the day of our meeting I knew he was far older than the character in the medieval tales who appears as a huntsman and psychopomp gathering the souls of dead warriors and is said to contain the fury of the spirits of Annwn within his person.

I felt like I'd met him before, had always known him, since time's beginning...

It was this soul-deep knowing that led me to devote myself to him as my patron god and to my becoming his awenydd, 'person inspired.'

Since then I've been journeying with Gwyn into his myths, learning the stories of other Inspired Ones who have served him, whose lives he has touched, whose souls he has gathered.

Peeling away the golden patina of the Christian scribes I have laid bare the atrocities Arthur and his men committed against the people of Annwn in order to overturn a worldview fundamental to our souls.

I have mourned Gwyn's forgetting in the Old North, as the Brythonic kingdoms fell and his stories were borne away to Wales, and perceived his absence and our disconnection from Annwn as a time of great soul-loss.

I have flown with the few who remembered him between sky and air.

With eyes wide with wonder I have witnessed Gwyn's return at the dawning of the Anthropocene to gather our souls back to him.

This book provides a record of my journey. It dismantles Arthurian mythology and is an invocation of a mythos ancient and new, offering reconnection with Annwn and inspiration to lead us into the next world.

Gwyn ap Nudd
Great God who is in our souls
and in whom we are gathered
I offer it to you.

I.
After the Ice Age

The Valley of Winter

*'Then the Ice Age came again and when it
retreated, even the shapes of the
hills and the names of the towns
in the valleys changed'*
 Joseph Delaney

My name is Snow. They say I am cold because I was born
in a snowstorm. We were all cold then, following the reindeer
north, following the North Star, following the instructions of
our ancestors on the margins of the Ice Age to the Valley of
Winter.

My earliest memories are the warmth of my mother's furs
and the furry bellies of our dogs. When she went hunting, she
left me to suckle at a bitch's teats. Mother and dog-mother
were indistinguishable. Both wore white-grey fur and had
luminous yellow eyes and sharp teeth, chewed my meat until
it was tender and spat it into my bawling infant mouth.

The only thing that distinguished dogs from wolves was
the octave of wildness in their howls. "One will suckle you
and one will eat you," my mother warned, "tear you apart like
a little white hare." At times like that I feared she might eat
me, her voice was so urgent and fierce.

I remember the blizzard plains and the comfort of our
little tent made from willow saplings and reindeer-skins. It
was like living in a reindeer's womb. When things were very
hard and there was no meat my mother fed me a stew of
stories instead.

She often recited How We Got Dogs: an old, old, story about how our Very Great Grandmother took in Nameless Grey's pups after their mother died in childbirth, nurtured them to health and trained them to hunt with us. Nameless Grey's descendants have never left our side.

In our getting of dogs my mother saw the will of our Winter God, who we knew by many names: White, Blessed, Holy, Wolf-Lord, Wolf-Skinned, The Hunter, Night-Time Footsteps Before Death, The Last Howl, Death-Eater, Gatherer of Souls, Lord of the Otherworld. She had her own secret name for him and told me one day I would have one too.

My mother believed Swift Paws was leading us to the Valley of Winter. Cupping my chin in her hand, she turned my face to hers so we touched nose-to-nose and I could see every wrinkle. "Our efforts will be worthwhile. We will be the first to reach our homeland. The herds know and the wolves follow. I perceive the guidance of our Far-Seeing Wolf-Eyed Lord."

We were a motley pack: ten dogs; three sleds; seventeen rangy, furred, roving humans urged onward with bites and nips and vociferous yowls of dream-vision from my mother. Five hunters with sapling-whittled spears for hunting reindeer, three huntresses with nets for catching snowy hares, another mother with a babe at breast, two girls, two boys, and Old Grey Hair who rode on the back of the sled. I didn't know who my father was then, although now I have my suspicions.

The further north we travelled the colder it got. One evening Old Grey Hair was found frozen as rigid as the men-in-the-boulders. We made a fire, straightened his limbs, laid him out with meat and a crowberry brew. Then my mother called to He Who Bites the Bonds to take him to the land where winters are never cold.

When we departed I did not look back nor did I look out of our tent. My mother had told me our Winter God, our God of Death, was so bright one look could blind you and that to look upon his face could drive you mad. She told me of the Mad Ones who fled to the mountains and ran with the wolves, how their ghosts joined his ghost-wolves hunting for souls.

I did not look, but I stayed awake and listened. As the full moon rose a howl shivered through the marrow of my bones, staked my near-stopped heart to my bed. I heard clandestine, snow-treading paws, a fearful wolf-melody on the wind from everywhere but nowhere.

The tent was illuminated by a piercing white light. I found myself adrift on another landscape, my fragile shelter, my very soul, becoming untethered. I clung to my furs, praying, apologising, terrified I was going mad until a wolf-shadow brought unconsciousness. When I awoke I was so cold I thought I was dead until I bit my wrist and tasted living flesh.

As we travelled into colder climes my people began to doubt my mother's sanity and our ancestors' instructions; the land had changed since they were driven south into exile by the glaciers. Even I believed my mother had succumbed to madness the night we camped on a precipice where our tents flapped in the icy wind like the wings of the Great Reindeer before she flew to the North Star.

That night I dreamt I was flying through a blizzard on a snowflake. We blew into a cave where there was an ancient woman with a large nose and thin grey hair. Her face was wrinkled as an old crowberry. She invited me to share a succulent reindeer-meat stew from an animal-skin cauldron and warm my hands at her roaring fire.

When I told my mother she exclaimed, "You have been gifted with a dream from our Winter God. That was our Very Great Grandmother. The Valley of Winter is not far away!"

True to her word, after we had climbed a seemingly endless ascent, knee-deep in snow, eyes stinging in the horizontal wind, we found ourselves looking down into a steep valley with stands of snow-clad birches and willows and a frozen river. "The White River," said my mother, "the valley may be deeper, the river less meandering, but they are still here. And look!" In the northernmost cliff face she pointed out the very same cave from my dream.

Our pack raced into the valley with triumphant howls. My mother and I headed for the cave to awaken the bones of our ancestors and make offerings to our Winter God at the White Spring.

Soon the thaw came, as foretold by our prophecies; the time when our Winter God surrenders our Goddess of the Land to our Summer God. The cracking of the ice is the breaking of his heart, the bursting of the White River his blood spilt to bring new life as the sacred marriage of Flame-Lipped and Heart's Desire births leaf and shoot.

Our pack celebrated all week yet my mother and I remained in the cave. As she told me, "There is ice in our blood. We do not thrive in summer."

When winter returned and the reindeer moved south, our pack followed, but we remained in the valley hunting snow-white hares and ptarmigan, foraging for mosses and lichens. Some days we survived on pure snow, growing light enough to ride on snowflakes.

My mother taught me to read messages from our Winter God in snowfall and cracks in ice and bone. I sat beside her as she opened the Wolf Bag (sewn from Nameless Grey's skin), cast the wolf-teeth, reindeer tarsal bones, birch and willow-bark; divined answers to her questions with our Very Great Grandmother's little finger bone.

When our pack returned, they sought her advice and very soon people from other packs were arriving with gifts of meat and drink in exchange for her wisdom. We seldom went hungry after that. (Of course, in our fortune, she saw the will of our Winter God).

Summers and winters passed. My mother took me to perform the rites of the dead, taught me to lay out bodies, speak the correct invocation of He Who Bites the Bonds. The bones of our pack were returned to the cave and arranged amongst the others with due ceremony.

When I got my blood, my mother told me of the blood magic: "Our blood is sacred because it links us to our ancestors and to our Winter God, who we have known since time's beginning. One drop can change the fate of the world as easily as a bleeding woman alters the course of the wind and summons hailstorms."

My mother died as she predicted, beneath the stars on a winter night, as she always wanted to. (She told me there's a point when the snow feels warm and that's when our Winter God takes you in his arms like our Dying Goddess and takes you away to the Otherworld.) She might have been ready to go with him, but I wasn't ready for her to depart.

I howled with the dogs and our howling summoned the ghosts of my ancestors. Tears freezing on my face, I lit a fire, unstiffened my mother's limbs, laid her out, placed beside her a few strips of dried meat, a cupful of birch-sap wine, and the paw of one of our faithful dogs.

I didn't want our Winter God to take her, but I knew I had no choice. Mustering my strength, I called to He Who Bites the Bonds, First Amongst Ghost Wolves, Knower of the Silver Ways, Gatherer of Souls. "Take my mother, Winter Dreamer, daughter of Winter Wanderer, daughter of Wolf-Led..." reciting the names of our ancestors back to our Very Great Grandmother, "to the winter that is never cold."

A wind whipped up. The ghosts disappeared. I walked away and did not look back, but heard the howling. I felt the bite, the bonds loosening, my throat unknotting, a weight lifting like a snowflake or a dream from my chest.

Three days afterward, I returned for my mother's bones and took them to the cave. I placed her skull on a shelf beside the skulls of all our grandmothers; her sternum, ribs, hip bones, thigh bones, finger bones... in their designated pits.

"You are with our ancestors now, Winter Dreamer, in the arms of our Winter God."

I was bitterly lonely without my mother, yet I never thought once about abandoning my position at the head of the Valley of Winter. My mother and I had always lived apart and life amongst the pack with its bickering and dog-fighting over mates had never appealed. I looked forward to their return, but not to summer.

To my consternation summers grew longer. Each year I counted more days between the thaw and first frost. The reindeer travelled further north. New plants and seedling trees appeared. I found out their names from my grandmothers: light-needled pine, blue-berried juniper, shivering aspen, tongue-like plantain, ragged dock, tawny sorrel, silver-flowered mugwort.

Every time I threw the contents of the Wolf Bag my Very Great Grandmother's little finger pointed to reindeer and trees moving north as Scorching Feet advanced. Why was Ice-Breathed allowing this to happen? Did he no longer care for his Beloved Maiden, or for me, Snow, who delights in his blizzard winds?

The year I feared the frosts would never come, I shouted from my cave, "Why have you deserted me, Winter Bringer? I've trained all my life to serve you. You took my mother, my grandmother, my great grandmother - all my mothers! And this is how you repay me: no snow, no blizzards, no reindeer. What kind of god are you?"

The wind rose and from it came the loneliest howl I had ever heard: a lost dog or wolf in terrible pain. Forgetting my worries, recalling my Very Great Grandmother's kindness to Nameless Grey, I descended from the cave and followed the outcry to the White River. The closer I grew, the quieter it got, ebbing to a whimper drowned by the rushing waters. I began to fear whatever was making it was dead.

Then, in a shadowy recess carved by the river, I saw it, sitting back on its haunches: a threadbare wolf with a human face. I stopped in my tracks. My mother had warned me about wolf-men, shapeshifters who preyed on women, but this was barely man-sized. Scrawny, bald, and shivering, it stunk of wet fur and its own excrement.

Lost in misery it did not look up until I touched the ragged tufts of its shoulder. The fur slid off to reveal the trembling near-skeletal body of a child. *It's no wolf-man, but a child brought up by wolves!* Snarling, it sunk its teeth into my arm, then scampered on all fours to the back of the recess and shivered harder.

Crying out in pain and surprise, I resisted the impulse to strike back. *It's afraid. I probably frightened it.* "I don't mean you any harm. Please don't waste your energy fighting. You need all you've got to stay alive."

It snarled again and bared its teeth. I noticed its nails were like claws. And straight on, how ugly its face was! Half its nose had been bitten away. A glimpse of a penis shrunken with cold disclosed its gender.

I dropped to all fours and whimpered softly. The wolf-boy's lip unsnarled. As our gazes met, I felt a flash of recognition, as if we'd met before. His eyes were yellow, feral, older than his physique suggested.

Slightly disconcerted, I spoke in whines and whimpers until I had won his trust. Eventually, he let me touch him, then wrap his stinking furs around him and carry him, too weak to struggle, back to the cave.

The dogs went crazy, greeting the wolf-boy with far more fervour than they'd ever greeted me. "Get off! Get down!" I admonished them as they leapt up gleefully, nearly knocking him over, drowning him in slobber. With a wolfish grin he fell to all fours and pushed his nose against theirs to avid tail wagging.

I lit the fire, warmed a reindeer-meat broth and set it in front of him with a spoon. Sitting on his haunches, he lapped it up, capered to me, licked my hand, then curled up and slept, his left leg occasionally twitching.

I slept uneasily, not used to the half-human, half-wolfish snores and grunts punctuating the sleeping-noises of the dogs. I was awoken at dawn by excited barking. Blinking as light streamed into the cave I heard scampering feet, then the wolf-boy appeared silhouetted against the entrance on all fours with a ptarmigan in his teeth. He deposited it beside me, spitting blood and feathers with a doting and expectant expression.

"Well, that will do for dinner at least." He watched puzzled as I plucked the bird and hung it over the fire. A glob of drool ran from the corner of his mouth down his chin and dripped onto the floor. He looked disappointed when he realised we wouldn't be eating soon.

His stench was putting me off all thought of food. "It's time you got a wash and clean furs." As I led him from the cave to the waterfall, I noticed the first frost had come, icing the brows of the men-in-the-boulders, sparkling on the branches of the trees. I took him down the steep path beside the stream to the waterfall.

He shivered and growled, but didn't bite me again when I removed his furs, doused him under the cold flood and, with a soap of tallow and ashes, scrubbed layers of filth from his skin and eased mats of dirt from his hair. I was surprised to find he was fair; he wasn't of our people. He shook himself off like a dog, then squatted with an accusing glare whilst I wrapped him in fresh furs and trimmed his nails.

Fed on rich meat stews and roots and tubers, he started to grow incredibly quickly. This may have been partly because he was learning to comport himself like a man rather than running on all fours. Nevertheless, it was disconcerting.

Slowly, he learnt language: "Meat," "water," "dog," "frost," "snow," "Snow," "fire." He seemed wholly unconcerned about his own identity and name. When I tried to teach him about our Winter God for the first time I heard him laughing: a tinkling sound like icicles, then a deeper roar like glaciers crashing.

When the thaw came and I taught him about the plants, I discovered he already knew their names. He learned to hunt and fight swiftly and outdid our pack when they returned to camp. Rumours abounded about our relationship. Of course it wasn't like that; he was just a boy, but at the rate he was growing, for how long?

One night I was certain I awoke with him lying beside me, his cock pressed against my hip. When I leapt up, he was fast asleep beneath his furs at the other side of the cave. Still, I told him it was time to find another sleeping place. He insisted on making his shelter just outside.

When I returned exhausted from a night-time confrontation with an angry spirit in a nearby camp, the wolf-boy was cooking breakfast, rotating the bird as I'd taught him. He might have looked civilized if it wasn't for the tell-tale blood stains on his teeth.

Pushing a plateful of ptarmigan into my hands with a fork, he sat beside me and put his arm round me. I stiffened. Yet his embrace was warm. I felt like I'd sat beside the fire with him before, had the sense that all my ancestors had sat beside him. For the first time since my mother died, I felt safe.

"Eat," he nuzzled my neck and pressed the fork into my hand. Once I had finished eating, I sank back into his arms and, before I knew it, was fast asleep.

I dreamt I was flying with the wolf-boy on a sled of ice pulled by a red-nosed dog and his team to the North Star to see the Great Reindeer.

Landing beside her tent-sized hooves, dwarfed by the hairy towers of her legs, looking up at her dexterous muzzle spitting star dust, "Why are you calling your children north?" I asked her.

"The reign of Winter is failing. Reindeer cannot survive where there is no snow."

"Snow and her pack cannot survive without reindeer. Is there no way you can send them back?"

The Great Reindeer's eyes were distant as nebulae as she shook her velvety antlered head.

"Look," the wolf-boy touched my shoulder and pointed to a land on the white, blue, and green earth. I noticed dark green trees advancing over the once icy plains toward the Valley of Winter. "With the forest will come new animals: elk, deer, boar, pine-martens, squirrels, woodland birds. There will be nuts and berries, no more hunger."

"Will it still snow?"

"Yes... there will be many hundreds more years of snow although your pack will not know them all."

"Why?"

"Summer is growing in power. In a Dark Age he will ally with a gristly tyrant with the soul of an old cave bear who despises Winter and death. When our sacred valley is seen as a place of wickedness and grief, Very Black, the last of your descendants, will be slaughtered for her blood."

"I will have descendants? How? When I've been brought up to live alone?"

The wolf-boy half-smiled.

"And my pack?"

"They will die without Inspired Ones and one day there will not be a single wolf in Prydain."

I gasped.

"Yet Very Black's blood will survive through the centuries to birth a new world where she and all her ancestors will be venerated and wolves will howl in the Valley of Winter again."

"How do you know this?" I asked confused. "Who are you?"

The wolf-boy took my hands in his. I found myself transfixed by his lambent eyes, unperturbed by his bitten face, his fangs, his lusty scent. His name was a bitter star to swallow. He sealed it down with a kiss and the knowing exploded inside me like when Old Mother Universe gave birth.

When I awoke the wolf-boy was gone. All he had left were his furs. There was no sign his shelter had ever been there. I prowled the cave, rubbed my nose in his scent, sat back on my haunches and howled.

A moon later, I did not get my blood. When the sickness started, I realised I was pregnant. The star in my belly had become a living child! This was the blessing and curse of all my ancestors. When I wept beside the White Spring my mother and all my grandmothers joined me. Our tears poured into the White River until it broke its banks.

So this is why the Valley of Winter will be known as the Valley of Grief.

My voice resounded from the cliffs. "I am Snow and without Winter I am nothing!"

Echoing back, "I am Winter and without Snow I am nothing!" A breath in my ear, then he was gone.

Yet he returned with the first frosts for the birth of our daughter. I named her Star Born, passed on my knowledge, our stories, the wolf-boy's prophecy. When she was prepared, I died in the arms of Winter.

Now I am snow.

Hunter in the Skies

There is a hunter in the skies
halloo halloo halloo
with a starlit bow and piercing eyes
halloo halloo halloo
a red-nosed hound is at his side
halloo halloo halloo.

The hunter gave me a dream.
The hunter gave him a dream.

I dreamed I carved a yew-wood bow
halloo halloo halloo
strung it taut with a dead man's sinew
halloo halloo halloo
then fletched an eagle-feathered arrow
halloo halloo halloo.

The hunter gave me a dream.
The hunter gave him a dream.

I dreamed I ran with a red-eared pack
halloo halloo halloo
antlered my brow and silent my tracks
halloo halloo halloo
the winter wind and moon at my back
halloo halloo halloo.

The hunter gave me a dream.
The hunter gave him a dream.

I dreamed I hunted a silver boar
halloo halloo halloo
with harrowing hooves and tusks like swords
halloo halloo halloo
who sixty chieftains felled and gored
halloo halloo halloo.

The hunter gave me a dream.
The hunter gave him a dream.

I dreamed I shot that silver boar
halloo halloo halloo
from his sterling side the red blood poured
halloo halloo halloo
yet still he charged with a wrathful roar
halloo halloo halloo.

The hunter gave me a dream.
The hunter gave him a dream.

I dreamed I pierced him with a spear
halloo halloo halloo
he rent my thigh with a red-tusked sneer
halloo halloo halloo
and we wrestled in a bloody mere
halloo halloo halloo.

The hunter gave me a dream.
The hunter gave him a dream.

I dreamed we fought nine nights and days
halloo halloo halloo
then like tides rolling back from the bay
halloo halloo halloo
in my arms he slipped away
halloo halloo halloo.

The hunter gave me a dream.
The hunter gave him a dream.

I dreamed I clutched a dragon lanced
halloo halloo halloo
a hawk, a pig, and snake in their death-dance
halloo halloo halloo
then in my arms I held a dead man
halloo halloo halloo.

The hunter gave me a dream.
The hunter gave him a dream.

I dreamed I killed a human soul
halloo halloo halloo
and woke up trembling stony cold
halloo halloo halloo

the hunter's truth fore'er to know
halloo halloo halloo.

The hunter gave me a dream.
The hunter gave him a dream.

Pack

Rolling, unfolding, through leaf and dirt, sometimes toothed, sometimes hoofed, sometimes horned, sometimes furred, sometimes feathered, sometimes clawed, sometimes winged, always fierce, we ran as one beast in many guises, we were one, we were Pack. We were followers of the Wolf Lord, the Antlered One, the Bowman of the Night, and in him were united.

Rolling, unfolding, through leaf and dirt on strong grey paws with my nose to the scent, tearing sinews, rending flesh, ripping out jugulars, the Hunter named me Wolf-Toothed. I was the Teeth of the Pack. Always in front in the hottest pursuit of prey. Always in charge at the campfire, renowned for my bloody jaws and never wiping my chin.

We as Pack were hunters and hunted. The Hunter taught this when we were cubs, squealers, fledglings, fawns, by hunting us with his hounds and shooting us down. He instilled in us a trembling reverence for the fear and pain of the hunted before we earned our weapons with feats of leaping, long nights of endurance, shooting straight through the heart.

We were hunted by those who were Not Pack. Those who lived in huts, tilled fields, gathered crops, herded animals, tied them up for slaughter. They chopped down and burned our forests so they could have more and more not-wild land, drove us north with our tails between our legs with flames and pitchforks and burning arrows.

When an arrow struck my shaggy grey flank, the flank of the Pack was wounded, thus the slowing of the Beast. When I died part of the Pack died. No Wolf-Toothed. No Teeth of the Pack. The Hunter took me to run with the Other Pack in the Other Forest where the Otherlight never dies. When I'd lost my old self he brought me back.

Rolling, unfolding, through leaf and dirt, bounding boundless through sapling and shrub with an uppity flick of my white tail, the Hunter named me Deer-Footed. I was the Feet of the Pack, the swiftest runner. As we hunted fleet-footed deer in antlered disguises I released fleet arrows into fleet hearts before the bucks moved in with spears.

I was blessed with two beautiful fawn daughters with quicker steps than me: the Beauty and Enchantment of the Pack with brown white-spotted hair and words of poetry. When I saw their white-tailed rumps in pools of blood I brayed and brayed. Vengeance came swiftly but did not make up for two hearts of the Pack forever erased.

We wandered without song in mourning accompanied only by harp-strings of trees in the wind. I never knew my third daughter. As I held her in my arms I bled unstanchably from something ruptured within. The Final Night crept in and from it stepped the Hunter to show me how she would run and sing and be the Prettiest of the Pack.

Rolling, unfolding, through leaf and dirt, I was Boar-Tusked, Elk-Antlered, Aurochs-Hoofed, Snake-Jawed, Raven-Winged, Squirrel-Tailed, Fox-Clever, Badger-Clawed; I was many parts, and one with the Beast. When the Hunter named me Owl-Eyed, I was the Eyes of the Pack, and this was the last and most painful of my manifold lives.

When the Pack was hunted into the last remnant of the forest I kept watch and hooted my warning, but was always too late. The wounded Beast was picked off one by one. I was left alone in my hole, no longer Pack, just a crazy owl kewicking over farmland, coughing up fossilised bones of sparrows and mice until my Last Dusk Flight.

I said to the Hunter, "I do not want to be reborn when there is no Pack." "Then hunt with me, Crazy Owl, join the Other Pack." He took me balanced on his wrist. Behind him I saw all my other selves, all the other selves of the Pack, united in one Beast to fly forever with the Hunter in the Skies, hunting down the starry souls, rolling, unfolding as Pack.

II.
The Purple-Cloaked Empire

The Dragon's Scream

'The... plague in your land.... that is a dragon, and a dragon of a
foreign people is fighting it... your dragon gives out a horrible scream'
   Lludd and Llefelys

What does a dragon's eye see?

I cast the contents of the Wolf Bag. Our Very Great
Grandmother's little finger bone points to the wolf's teeth
marking battles, the reindeer tarsal bones where each fortress
will be built. Where my ancestors saw trees advancing north I
see an unstoppable army.

A century ago the Romans were blown from our island by
a wintry storm. Now they have returned with their ships, their
catapults, their impenetrable shield walls. The inexorable
thump of their marching feet is getting closer and closer to
the Valley of Winter.

I know I could be safe here in this cave, with my herbs and
bones, with my grandmothers. Yet I cannot rest for the dead
crying out on the wind, knowing the Gatherer of Souls trawls
the battlefields.

I have followed where he gathers those crushed beneath
chariots by catapult balls, impaled by sword and spear,
trampled beneath the boots of the legions, and, possessed by
their fury, possesses our warriors as Wolf of War, Bull of
Battle, Eagle of Strife, striking blows beyond their strength
and surviving wounds beyond their endurance.

I have seen our people fighting in his battle-fog and his
hand pulling them from the fog.

My heart has broken countless times; for them, for him. I have tried to help him sing back the lost, near lost myself where battles have torn the veil between the worlds, the newly-dead wander traumatised, and the Furious Ones he holds back attempt to pour forth.

When I was gifted my name, Wind Singer, I dreamed of singing in a time when the tribes lived in peace. On summer nights I strewed meadowsweet throughout my cave and sang from dusk until dawn. Now I lay its sweet-smelling flowers on the chests of the corpses, thrown without rites into mass graves, and keen and weep.

My hopes are dying on the winds born from the abyssal cavern where I was conceived. The dragons have abandoned the well in the Otherworld from which the Song of the Universe is born.

Forty years ago I was taken there by the Walker Between Worlds. I thought he was just another ghost until he downed his shield and sword, rubbed off his woad, on unseen wings showed me the secret paths of the winds and the caves of colossal bones.

Deep beneath the earth where stone melts into darkness he guided me like a leaf across a black sea to the well from which new-born stars emerge, singing their beginnings, surrounded by new worlds.

Beside it slept two dragons: one red, one white. Their scaly flanks rose and fell slowly as the growth and decay of mountains. The four winds blew steadily from the immense caverns of their nostrils.

In the slumber of those mighty beings I felt such beauty and peace I wanted to prostrate myself before them and would have died there and then, knowing my life had been worth living for that moment.

Yet He Who Knows Dragons was determined to show me other wonders. He took me to the brink of the well where we tumbled into dragon-reflections. I arose red-winged with a belly full of fire and he white-winged with trails of ghosts steaming from his nose.

I recall only glimpses of magma, hot winds, ice-topped mountains, melting glaciers, trees taller than giants; our final intertwining flight, him whispering his name into my dragon's ear. I still do not know why he taught me what a dragon's eye sees.

When we returned I heard my name singing from the well with others more confusing: "Wind-Singer, Dragon-Singer, Singer of the Dragons' Cradle, Singer of the Dragons' Sleep, Singer at a World's End."

Had I seen the dragons stir then? The red opening her golden eye? The white twitching his tail?

I named my baby girl and boy, my beautiful twins, after those great powers, hoping they would soar too: Flame Red and Ghost White.

I began to regret it the next night: the eve of Claudius' invasion. My babes began to wail and, in a deep cavern at the back of my mind, I heard talons scraping stone, unfolding wings, mighty roars, earth shuddering as those otherworldly forces broke free.

The prophecies of my ancestors had foretold the dragons would awaken at a time of great strife, possessed by the fury of our people and our enemy, and a plague would fall upon Prydain.

I was aware of them battling over every battlefield where I walked with the Guide of the Slain; scales torn by tooth and claw, wings rent, showers of dragon's blood pooling in footprints of dead warriors.

Their rage infected my children who squabbled and vied for my favour. The day I returned to find them scratched and bruised, Flame Red standing over Ghost White with a dagger proclaiming she would take my position before he leapt for her throat, I separated and exiled them.

"Do not come back," I spoke sternly although I was being torn apart, "until you are prepared to work together as caretakers of the Valley of Winter and the ways of our Lord of the Otherworld in peace."

I closed my ears to the reports on the wind for fear that in my weakness I would beg my dragon-babies, my red and white-haired darlings, my pretty-faced savage monsters, to return.

Over my anguish rang the red dragon's scream as she lost to the white dragon. Her deafening, spine-chilling, heart-shrivelling vociferation gave voice to the fury of all the people of Prydain, living and dead, as they surrendered their land and freedom to the Romans.

It was so terrifying warriors lost their strength and colour, sunk to their knees with their hands clamped over their ears and died curled up in foetal positions. Youths leapt from cliff tops or took knives to their wrists. Pregnant women cried out at the cramp in their bellies and, hours later, mournfully buried their chick-like babes in secret pits. Misshapen calves and foals did not last a day. Fish flapped and floundered on the banks of dried up rivers and birds fell from the air. Plants withered, leaves fell from trees, crops failed. The Roman senators grew fat on imported goods whilst our people starved.

I walked with my god as he gathered the lost souls. "Can't you stop it?"

Grimly he shook his head. "I have known the fury of the spirits of the Otherworld so long I no longer know peace. I am that fury."

I didn't want to believe him, but in my soul I knew he spoke the truth: a part of him was the furore and terror that caused those deaths just as a part of him gathered the dead with love and compassion.

"Yet you still know peace," he continued, "I felt it when we danced through the skies as dragons."

What does a dragon's eye see?

As I look down on the contents of the Wolf Bag a cloud passes overhead, casting a shadow over my divining, and the ptarmigan feathers flutter up on the wind like departing souls. "A plague," I whisper.

The dragon's scream rings in my ears like tinnitus. I know the High Ones, the Vigorous Ones, the Deep Ones, the Stag People, the Horse People, the Wind People have fallen. The Romans have arrived in the wild lands of the North and with them the plague approaches.

"Wind Singer, Wind Singer!" the spirits come to pull me away to sing back the dead.

When I arrive on the battlefield the Gatherer of Souls looks weary. He has downed his shield and leans on his spear as he sings the soul-names. As I prepare to join my voice with his, he shakes his head.

"Look up."

I do not want to, but his fingers grip my chin, forcing me to behold the red dragon coughing phlegm and blood from exposed lungs, organs pumping red against the darkness of the starless night.

The skull of the white dragon has been exposed by tearing claws and his right eye is an empty hollow. Yet he is lashing his tail, fixing the red with a left eye burning with hatred, preparing for a killing blow.

I cannot close my eyes to the horror as the white dragon tears out the entrails of the red, unravelling her being in infinite folds, falling, falling, falling to the earth to become a wyrm with a snapping head wrapping around his bony body to bear him down.

I watch in despair as they swallow one another like whales and are spat from each other's stomachs, feed like sharks, smash hammer heads, fight like stags with interlocking antlers, stallions with round hooves and gnashing teeth, gristly sharp-tusked boars.

"She is the spirit of Prydain and he is her Other," the White Warrior reveals. "You are the only one with the inspiration of the winds of the Otherworld and the peace within who can sing them back."

"How?"

"I... don't know... their fury tears me apart." He dissipates into the ghosts.

I want to scream for fear of losing him, but know it will join the dragon's scream; my soul, his soul, thus all souls and the world will be lost.

Instead I begin to sing and the first song on my lips is a lullaby passed down from Snow that once brought rest to my squabbling twins:

Sleep babes sleep
daddy's gone a hunting
he'll bring us snowy white hares
and ptarmigan; in his wolf furs
we're so safe and warm.

Sleep babes sleep
daddy's gone into the cold again
he'll bring us a white bushy-tailed
snow fox; in his wolf furs
we're so safe and warm.

Sleep babes sleep
daddy's gone into the frost again...

As I sing I notice the dragons, still in the shapes of boars, are ceasing their battle. Facing each other, distant as planets, their deep-set gazes meet then drop. Sprouting wings they spiral downward, becoming smaller as they approach: boisterous juveniles, stripy squealers, tiny piglets.

They fall into my arms. As I cradle them just like I held the twins they become red-haired and white-haired babes. Tears of wonder pour down my cheeks as I sing the last verse of the lullaby:

Sleep babes sleep
daddy's gone into the snow again
he'll bring us the last reindeer
of the North; in his wolf furs
we're so safe and warm.

I feel the presence of our Winter God in the shivering of my skin. He hands me a pair of wolf furs to wrap them in and looks down fondly.

"How can this be?" I whisper in awe. "How can they be dragons, the spirit of Prydain and her Other, the twins, and us?"

For a moment I am the red dragon and he the white soaring through the blue and boundless skies aware of the immensity of our love and its potential to turn into the deadliest hatred.

My reverie is interrupted by sharp teeth nibbling furs and a thrashing tail. "Quickly", he says, "we must return them to the Womb of Old Mother Universe before they return fully to themselves."

We rush down through the caverns of the Otherworld to the deepest place. There I rock the dragons back to sleep and lay them beside the well.

"Wind-Singer, Dragon-Singer, Singer of the Dragons' Cradle, Singer of the Dragons' Sleep, Singer at a World's End."

I understand all my names but the last.

"The Age of Iron and War is over and we are entering the Age of the Purple-Cloaked Empire," explains He Who Sees Into The Waters.

With a weary sigh he continues, "In the Dark Age when Romanised men claim lordship not only over Prydain, but over the Otherworld, the dragons will reawaken. Once Very Black, the last of your lineage, lies dead there will be no Inspired Ones to put them to sleep."

"Will you ever know an end to the fury?" I feel exhausted, too, and old.

Instead of answering he replies, "There are two people approaching the Cave of the Ancestors. One is a red-haired woman in warrior garb and the other a white-haired man in robes."

"Flame Red and Ghost White!" I exclaim.

I depart on the winds to greet my children, returning from exile, with their promise to take my position together and live in peace.

The Chalk God

'The final pit I will mention is a recent discovery and is exciting in that within it was an underground shrine associated with a chalk sculpture, perhaps of a chthonic deity'
  Miranda Green

There are things beneath the earth. I see them in my dreams. My little sister was one of them. Mother buried her in the corner of our hut. She waited for us. Out of the corner of my eye I saw her sucking her thumb, giving us a little wave, pushing up to toddle and falling back down.

I wanted to one step two step with her. I wanted to teach her the words for 'dog' and 'horse' and 'cow' and 'wheat.' I wanted to see her growing up, but she was stuck in her second year, repeating the same motions, whilst I learnt to clean hides, sew, and ride a pony. In my dreams I made her corn doilies and watched her shaking a cow-skin rattle filled with seeds.

I cursed myself for getting mad at her for drooling, crying, and soiling her sheets. I said "sorry" until there were no more s's within me. We didn't know she was ill until the fever took. At night I can still smell her sickness curdling with the sweetness of my mother's herbs: feverfew, yarrow, elderberry, meadowsweet. I can still hear her prayers to the Mother Goddesses for healing.

When her efforts failed my mother feared the wrath of the spirits of the Otherworld. She went to the Chalk God and came back paler than him, biting her lip, tears welling in her eyes like huge dewdrops, then collapsed sobbing in my father's arms. That night my little sister died.

Children weren't meant to go down to the Chalk God. We weren't supposed to know about him, but we did. Our parents spoke of him when the wheat did not grow or the seed went rank in the pits, when diseases struck, madnesses, untimely deaths. At those times the priests went down with offerings and placations. They didn't go down much apart from that.

It was rumoured that if children went down they came out blind or their hair fell out or their fingers fell off, that Happy's hair was white because he went to the Chalk God and that was why he was a little mad and found the world so funny. My mother certainly hasn't been the same since.

I used to wonder who he was and if he was lonely and if he was truly wicked enough to cause those terrible things. After Gold Hair died (I still struggle to speak her name) I wanted someone to blame and the most obvious person was the Chalk God.

I nurtured a hatred of him, like a pyre, onto which I threw my sorrow, my anger, my guilt, my bitterness, the loss of both my sister and a part of my mother who would never sing with such lightness or smile so easily again.

Each tiny thing - each delay in the wheat ripening, each broken stalk and blackened husk, each cough or cold, cut or graze, I blamed on him and thus the pyre grew within me.

The other children saw it in my eyes. They no longer wanted to play. Good. I no longer wanted to play with them.

My pony shied from me. I slapped her and pulled down on her reins. She ditched me. I gave up riding. I plunged my needle in and out of the skins in a furore imagining it was the Chalk God's skin and got the sinew all tied up. Told to start again, I threw my work down and trampled it into the floor and stormed out. When Gold Hair recoiled from me I shouted at her then, as she faded away, shouted at myself, and then at my mother.

My father tossed me kicking and screaming into bed without supper. I sobbed all night cursing every single mistake I'd made and feeding them to the pyre. I decided there would be no more mistakes. I was going to confront the Chalk God. I was going to make him feel my pain. I was going to win back my sister from his underground realm, then I was going to kill him.

To find out where he was I needed to cause a calamity. It came to me clear as daylight: I needed to destroy the wheat. Gold Hair tugged at my trouser leg as I snuck out of our hut at midnight. I feared her sobbing would wake the village, but nobody listens to dead children anymore.

Beneath the light of the full moon I danced like a demented spirit. Trampling down the wheat-heads I shouted out to the Chalk God, "Is this how you feel when you destroy our crops? Is this how you felt when you cut my sister down with your harrowing blade?"

I'd never felt so good as when I stomped away with clods of mud sticking to my boots with strands of wheat, took them off, clapped them together.

I'd never felt so bad as when I turned and looked back to see the trampled fields, the broken stalks, the fallen ears of wheat, wispy bearded ghosts rising from them, and pale spirits at work gathering them up and tucking them into carry-sacks. Looking down from the moon I saw the Chalk God's implacable face and for the first time knew pure terror. A cold wind blew my pyre out and I was left shivering in the utter awfulness of him and of my deed.

"He made me do it," I told myself when I awoke and when the news broke around the village.

"It's as if a party of otherworldly spirits..."

"A death dance..."

"A curse..."

No-one could have guessed it was the doing of a nine-year-old girl.

The priests drew everyone together. A calf was sacrificed and burnt so his ashes could be taken in a special white urn down to the Chalk God.

As their procession left and the villagers returned to work I claimed sickness then scrabbled and wormed out of the back of our hut. I ran behind the middens and caught sight of the priests beyond the broken fields going over a hill. I followed to its summit and saw them disappear into a grove.

"So it's in there. The underground abode of the Chalk God." As I whispered those words a breeze chilled me and I was overcome by an inexplicable choking feeling.

After I'd wriggled back into our hut I really felt sick. When mother and father returned and I couldn't eat they exchanged concerned glances and I felt sicker at their fears of a second bereavement.

"It will all be alright when I've done away with the Chalk God," I muttered to myself.

"Pardon?" said my mother.

"Nothing," I snapped.

"Fi, Fi," Gold Hair reached out her little hands imploringly and shook her golden locks. Her eyes were big and dark and full of innocence.

Ignoring her I stomped away to bed and lay there until darkness was well fallen and the waning moon lit the sky.

Once more I snuck away, this time heading for the smithy to get the hammer to smash the Chalk God to smithereens.

As an owl hooted over the barren fields I felt a slither of guilt, but blamed it once more on the Chalk God. Hefting the hammer I practiced blows, imagining smashing his face to keep other thoughts out.

Yet as I approached the grove I realised tears were streaming down my cheeks. It was hard enough to see in the shadows of the trees as I scrabbled for the planks that covered the entrance without that blurry flood. My tummy was tight. My lungs were heaving in and out like the bellows of the Roman disaster engine I had seen in a dream.

As I pushed the planks away a cold draught blew up from the underworld and stole my breath. I felt as if I was gasping with the sadness of all the mothers and fathers and sisters and brothers who'd lost children.

"His fault." I threw down the hammer. It landed with an echoing bang. Nearly satisfying.

I drew a candle from my pocket and lit it with flints and gripped it determinedly between my teeth as my toes then my fingers found the footholds carved into the hard earth and I went down to the Chalk God.

When I'd descended three times my height my feet touched solid ground and I spun round. There he was. Not half as big as I'd imagined, in a niche at the back of the chamber with a too-perfectly round head, square eyes, and a very long slender neck like a swan's on a stub body.

He'd be gone in one blow. Smashing him would almost be sad. I shook off that thought. As I downed the candle and picked up the hammer a shiver of foreboding ran through me like wind through rain.

"Fi, Fi," I heard Gold Hair cry.

The hammer slithered in my sweaty hands.

"You need to let her go." The Chalk God's voice was disarmingly kind.

The tears rose again and I drove them back down with the pain that I'd stored up for him. "You killed her. I'm not going to let you take her soul away!"

"I understand your sorrow."

"You know nothing of how I feel!"

"I have felt the sorrow of all souls returning from your world to mine."

As the Chalk God spoke I found myself standing in a void surrounded by grieving women and men, boys and girls, "I lost my baby girl," "I lost my boy," "my little sister should have been my best friend. We were going to have so many adventures together." "We should have caught rabbits and lit campfires and counted every single one of the stars".

Horrified by the onslaught of voices I tried to push them away. I noticed the Chalk God was getting more distant, fading into a speck of white light. Realising he was the only one who could hold them back, I tried to reach out to him, but my arm was not long enough. It was like reaching for a star. "Don't go. Please don't leave me with them!"

The bereaved ones dissipated. Then I heard the laughter of children. They approached hand-in-hand, in a line, walking on air, balancing gleefully chuckling toddlers between them. They headed toward three plump women who gathered them into their arms and kissed their foreheads.

"Fire Wind, let her go with the Children of the Otherworld."

"Fi?" I saw Gold Hair in our hut staring at the ghostly children with eyes bright with longing.

Tears. I'd held on to her for so long. Since the minute she'd died. Since her burial. Since she'd reappeared in our hut. I'd literally held on to those soft little hands and wanted to be the one to walk her and now he expected me to hand her over to these spirits with whom she could dance.

I saw the rightness and a part of me wanted to be that young again and to be kissed by one of the Mothers.

She blew me a kiss...

"What will become of me?" I finally realised the last few years of my life had centred on Gold Hair's death; on nurturing my hatred for the Chalk God who I didn't hate anymore.

"Live."

"But how... after the terrible thing that I did..." I recalled the wheat field. "Will you let me come to you? Will they?"

I assumed he knew I referred to the Roman priests who had taken our freedom.

"I am far bigger than a statue," spoke the Chalk God. "It does not contain me. Neither does this cavern. I am deep within the land and deep within your soul. These mysteries, that children's tales and the lessons of priests do not touch upon, I will teach you."

"You will? Even after the... wheat?"

"I understand."

Thinking back to how I had danced like an otherworldly spirit I knew he did.

I released Gold Hair and wriggled back into our hut. The anger left me and I began to understand about things beneath the earth and dreams and that path has been mine ever since. They closed the shrine to the Chalk God and filled it in, but I did not lament because he is more than that. Still, that's how I see him, with his swan's neck, bearing the souls of our people away.

After Procopius

'In the island of Britain the men of ancient times built a long wall...
on the north side... it is actually impossible for a man to survive there
even half an hour, but countless snakes and serpents and every other
kind of wild creature occupy their area as their own'
  Procopius

North of the Wall I am running
from Roman civilisation
from the ones who build straight roads
from the ones who stand in line.

North of the Wall I am running
to greet my madness
a whirlwind of serpents at my heels
torn-out leaves in my hair.

North of the Wall I am running
amongst mad women
streaking bare through the forest
shedding my second skin.

North of the Wall I am running
with every wild creature
a halo of birds around my coming
open-beaked with soaring wings.

North of the Wall I am running
with the hunger of the wolf-pack
howling and slithery-jawed
erupting into fur and paw.

North of the Wall I am running
with the madness of gwyllon:
shadowed men who come as wolves
the greater shadow of Annwn's lord.

North of the Wall I am running
until I don't want to run any more.
In our grove of pine there is silence
and the heartbeat of steady awe.

North of the Wall I stop running
and turn to face my challengers:
roads running on forever
countless rows of spears and shields.

From North of the Wall I return
cloaked in feather and claw.
To breach the gap
and bring down the divide

I am running back from the Wall.

III.
The Dark Age

The Madness of Goleuddydd

'from the hour she became pregnant she went mad'
  Culhwch and Olwen

Goleuddydd ran. Far from the town, far from her husband's quarters, far from her husband's bed. Cilydd Lord of Celyddon was a monster. His semen glinted on her naked thigh as she ran pell-mell into the moonlit forest, heedless of the scratchy twigs, the flutter of woken birds.

She should have known the ways of men. Her sister, Eigr, had told her how she had seen Uther Pendragon's lustful gaze in her husband's eyes before he got her with her tyrant child, Arthur.

The boar-like Cilydd had treated Goleuddydd like a sow to be bred. She'd broken from the pen. When her trembling legs would carry her no further and her breath burned like wildfire in her chest she sank down, wracked by sobs that shuddered through the trees like a hurricane. She pulled at her hair, raked at her skin, rolled in the dirt and pine needles, longing to be a thing of the forest and not a woman with memories that haunted her more relentlessly than ghosts.

"Not Goleuddydd. Not Goleuddydd." She repeated the negation of her name as tears poured down her muddy face like swollen streams and she rocked like a stone with her knees hugged to her chest.

The forest creatures gathered to look at this stranger creature. Mice crept up and preened their whiskers nervously. Their darting glances asked what her pain-filled noises meant. Squirrels scrambled along branches and flicked their red tails. The mice fled as a white wolf approached with saliva dripping from his jaws.

Goleuddydd was so lost in her misery, reliving her husband's approach, his heavy hands bruising her flesh, that she did not see the wolf prowling around her in smaller and smaller circles.

Halting, he growled, "Not Goleuddydd."

Her memories dissipated like mist. Suddenly she was aware of only the gnarled pines and blaeberry bushes silvery and shadowy in the moonlight, the low whisper of the wind, the sharp scent of pine needles and earthier dirt, the feral presence of the wolf before her.

"Run with me."

Fine grey hairs erupted on the backs of her hands and thickened rapidly. Her fingernails yellowed and twisted into claws. She fell onto all fours shaking her ruff and flexing snarly jaws.

Her senses expanded. How intense the scents of a myriad prey her wolf-knowing identified as deer, rabbit, mouse, of the wolf's musk. A fierce hunger seared her belly, not just for the taste of meat, but the thrill of hunting in this limber body alongside her companion.

She touched her snout to the wolf's and they leapt together into a world of needle-strewn scent-paths, blood-pumping chases and kills, tearing flesh, gnawing bone, guzzling marrow. Each night they slept warm and satiated, thick coats touching, beneath a blanket of stars and pine.

For nine months she ran with the wolf. When her pregnancy reached its end he took her to the edge of the forest and downed a young doe as their final meal.

Once they had eaten, he raised his bloody jaws. "Goleuddydd."

She fell out of her wolf's skin into a taller, pinker form, belly stretched and round as the full moon, breasts swollen and heavy as a sow's udders and dripping with milk.

As Goleuddydd's contractions began she stumbled from the forest, her hand on the wolf's ruff, as he guided her toward a pig-run where she piled the straw into a nest and lay gasping as memories of the man whose son she bore flooded back to her.

She fought desperately to ward them off with thoughts of her brilliant, moon-chased nights with the wolf. Yet the stars, the prey, the softness beneath his savagery, could not break through the physicality of giving birth to the horrible little squealing thing with skinny limbs, pig's ears, and an upturned snout.

Pushing aside her horror she took him in her arms and pulled him to her breast. As he suckled greedily she spoke softly, "Because you were born in a pig-run I shall name you Culhwch, my slender piglet."

Leader of the Hunt I

*'Twrch Trwyth will not be hunted until Gwyn son of Nudd is found.
God has put the fury of the devils of Annwn in him, lest the world be
destroyed. He will not be spared from there'*
    Culhwch and Olwen

Their fury within me is like a battlefield without end.

I had known battles between men, but not of the men of
the world turning from the gods to one God against the
ancients of Prydain.

It began with a crash of lightning over a hilltop fortress and
the flash of knives across the throats of the nine gatekeepers
and nine mastiffs who guarded the nine gates to its nine
towers. As their blood poured out, their knees weakened, and
their vision failed I was called to them.

My hand trembled as I closed the wounds of the gristled
old guardians who had watched over the abode of
Ysbaddaden Bencawr, Head of Giants, for centuries. Their
single unblinking eyes had once seen everything and I had
delighted in solving their near-insolvable riddles.

As I took their veiny hands, near-fleshless in old age, and
pulled out their souls, they mumbled in senility about mists
and flowers and stars and the workings of the universe.
Gaping down on their bodies they could scarcely believe the
final answer to their questions was death.

"Impossible!"

"Who would dare this?"

Clasping their staffs they recanted their spells.

Stooping to rouse the souls of the heavy-headed mastiffs, I pulled gently on their velvety ears. They rose with growls, teeth bared, saliva dripping from wobbly jaws, eyes lighting like pools of magma.

I led them into the shadows of the hall of the Head of Giants. Ysbaddaden sat stooped at a cliff-high table. His once formidable frame was emaciated. His hands, huge as calves, were palsied and useless. His beard was brittle and tangled as a dying hawthorn bush. A team of six men with pitchforks held open the heavy lids of his rheumy eyes.

Before him stood the murderers with blood on their hands and bloody knives sheathed. I recognised Arthur's warband by their dragon flag and Arthur's cousin, Culhwch, at their fore in an ostentatious purple cloak carrying a gold-chased shield and gold-hilted sword.

As lightning crackled up the gatekeepers' staffs and the mastiffs snarled I held back their fury.

I set my teeth as Ysbaddaden toothlessly mumbled the forty impossible tasks Culhwch must fulfil to win his daughter, Olwen; giving away the names of his kindred, the ancient animals, the treasures of Annwn, my hounds and huntsmen.

When he betrayed my name I dragged my onslaught of premonitions with the scandalised gatekeepers and mastiffs back to Annwn.

Two of Arthur's warriors played dice on Pumlumon to decide the order of the tasks.

What should have been done by cunning will be done by slaughter.

I was called by the death cry of Dillus Farfog to find his trunk buried neck deep in a pit, beside it his severed head with blood oozing from every pore of his chin. Beside it the instruments of torture - a pair of foot-long wooden tweezers - were set aside neatly like a knife and fork after a pleasant meal. Reaching into the blood-soaked soil for his soul, I grasped his gargantuan hand in two of mine.

The once-proud giant wept like a baby. "They plucked out my beard strand by strand whilst I lived because it would be brittle when I was dead. They boasted they were going to weave it into a leash for a hound of Annwn."

I nearly choked on my outrage.

Soon afterward I was called to the naked corpse of Rhitta Gawr; headless, beardless, stripped of his cloak of beards; to Diwrnarch Gawr, Cribwr Gawr, Maelor Gawr, Benlli Gawr...

Across Prydain giants lay headless and beardless, stony limbs scattered in fragments on their hilltops. I helped them pull themselves together, fixed their broken fingers, stuck on their peeled-off fingernails, guided their spirits into Annwn's craggy beds and chairs.

Their anger gathered into a muttering beneath the land that sounded like grinding rocks as Arthur and his men set forth to capture my hounds with leashes woven from their bloody beards.

As Prydwen cut through the waves of Aber Daugleddyf, I swam down, shook myself off in the sea-cave where Rhymi lay with two suckling whelps, barked my warning. They rose to fight with affronted snarls, biting off arrows, barging the ship.

When I saw the rows of warriors waiting at the harbour I barked again, but still they were driven toward the wall of shields. Weakened by arrows, pierced by spears, they were captured, leashed, forced to throw off their wet grey coats and take human form.

Aned and Aethlem - swift as a gust of wind - were lassoed from the skies in spite of my barking at their heels.

I lent my strength to Drudwyn yet he was leashed and dragged snarling from his den.

I was with the Dog Heads in every bite, relishing the taste of blood, spitting blood when they tasted death and was rendered speechless as Arthur's men cut off their heads and sliced out their tongues.

I fought again with Gwrgi Garwlwyd who was slaughtered and stripped of his rough grey hide.

When Arthur went after my huntsmen a blood-stained leash of foreboding closed around my neck.

I asked the Oldest Animals to remain silent about Mabon, but they claimed a deeper wisdom. (Only the Toad of Cors Fochno played mum, pretending to choke on the lump in his throat).

The Blackbird of Cilgwri, Stag of Rhedynfre, Owl of Cawlwyd, and Eagle of Gwernabwy guided Arthur's men to the Salmon of Llyn Lliw. That damned fish, thinking he was so wise, carried them on his spiny back upriver to Mabon's house of stone beneath Caer Loyw.

I fought alongside the Nine Witches who guarded the Sun Child's tomb as the sting in their swords, the swiftness in their knives, the swing in their fists, the ice in their spells, the bite in their final prophecies.

When Arthur's warriors split their heads the witches spat from cloven mouths: "You forget we trained you." "We made you." "You will be nothing without us." "Empty knights." "Heartless." "Soulless." "Without magic." "We have foreseen your end."

The wall between the worlds fell and both were flooded by blinding light as Mabon was piggy-backed away.

I lent Cynedyr Wyllt nine times the wildness of the wildest beasts on the mountains yet he was leashed.

When Arthur captured Bwlch, Cyfwlch, and Syfwlch, who are destined to blow their horns at the end of the world, I saw quaking lands, falling skies, rising seas, and a deafening roaring filled my ears.

I was appalled to see the warriors of Prydain kneeling before Arthur, the great god Amaethon ploughing his fields, Gofannon setting the plough.

Gwythyr's father then Gwythyr bent his knee. My cursed rival walked his daughter, Gwenhwyfar, down the aisle to marry Prydain's King. With the aid of ants he retrieved the flax seed for Olwen's veil.

On Nos Galan Gaeaf when I slew Gwythyr I gave vent to my rage as I cut him down like a sheaf of corn with my harrowing blade, ripped him limb from limb, strewed his blood across the fields of Prydain.

When I gathered Creiddylad into my arms her pallor reminded me of the night I promised never again to release the fury of my spirits.

Standing between Gwythyr and I on a blackened battlefield with tears streaking her cheeks Creiddylad said, "I will stay with each of you for six months if you stop wreaking destruction on Thisworld and Annwn."

When Gwythyr agreed and I did not answer, "I will die for you," she spoke sincerely.

"I promise," I whispered.

Creiddylad kissed me once before paling and passing to Annwn.

For the first time since that night I was roused from our bed by the blazing agony of trees. From the window of my fortress I saw fire on the horizon: Gwythyr, back from the dead! Negating his promise to Creiddylad, the trust I'd placed in him, despite our enmity.

Shaking Creiddylad awake, "Gwythyr has betrayed us both. How dare he assault my world?!"

I departed like thunder to blow my horn and muster my spirits against Gwythyr and his host. We rode forth as a blizzard against their burning swords and froze them into the burnt-out waste. I channelled my fury into making Gwythyr pay as we fought with sword-blows, then with teeth as wolf and lynx, then as intertwining serpents.

When I'd near squeezed the life from him, "Why?" I demanded. "Why have you broken our pact?"

"The people of Prydain don't want winter... death... anymore," he choked. "The time approaches when Creiddylad will be freed from imprisonment in Annwn... forever in my arms... an eternal summer..."

With a determined wriggle he slipped from my grasp and resumed human form. His golden hair was matted with blood, his right eye swollen closed; blood from a myriad wounds mottled his furs.

Recalling how his golden eyes had once been filled with sunlight and laughter and light I thought with regret of how we'd been the closest of friends and of our descent into bitterest hatred.

Through split lips he spat, "Soon you will be dead beyond return and there will be a new Leader of the Hunt."

"Never!" I thrust my sword through Gwythyr's chest, then hacked until he was nought but frozen chunks of flesh.

Only seven of his men lived. I threw them into my coldest prison and when Nwython assaulted me I slammed him against the wall, breaking every bone in his body, and ripped out his heart.

"So you never forget the price for breaking into my realm," I handed it, still beating, to Cyledyr, his son.

The blonde fay-looking youth juggled the slippery organ in trembling long-fingered hands.

"Within my pack there is a rite by which ancestral knowledge is passed on from father to son," I told him. "Eat it and your father's wisdom will be yours."

Cyledyr paled and retched.

"Eat it or I will," I bared my blood-stained teeth.

Cyledyr sobbed and gagged as he ate it then frenetically licked his bloody fingers.

He will become wyllt. I saw it in his eyes. I knew it in my gut. I thought back to my own times of madness and of the fury within me that threatens to madden all the people of the world.

As Calan Mai approached my strength faded. I kissed farewell to Creiddylad and thus to life as Gwythyr returned golden-haired with swallows for heralds and raised his fiery sword to bathe Annwn in a pink dawn.

Behind him rode Arthur and his men, galloping through my burnt-out forest, shooting down its defenders, stealing cattle from my plains, assaulting my guards, and wresting the Men of the North from my prison.

They crowded into my feast, culling my music, overturning my tables, slaughtering my people, who had barely begun their plates of roast pork and apple or touched their mead. We fought against a shipload of men and, when they were dead, against two shiploads more.

To my grief my fair folk fell with battered heads, holes in their chests, bowels spilling out amongst toppled fruits, blood mixing with honey-gold.

The living will bring death to Annwn.

Arthur's men encircled me with innumerable swords. I parried and struck a dozen times as fast as any man, felling dozens and surrounding myself with a circle of corpses. For each death I took a blow.

I fell bleeding from countless stinging wounds, collapsed hamstrung, dropping my sword as they severed the tendons in my sword-arm.

The dead will rise again.

I had lived this scene in recurring nightmares and heard over it the voices of the fates.

"Gwythyr please," Creiddylad pleaded for my swift end. She looked astoundingly beautiful in her hawthorn blossom crown although her lips were pressed and her brow was furrowed by a frown.

Gwythyr unforgivably looked from his bride-to-be to Arthur.

Arthur called his men back, stepped between us, and drew his sword. It was engraved with two serpents, who leapt into life, breathing fire from their jaws. "By the might of Caledfwlch, I, Arthur Pendragon, hereby make peace between Gwyn and Gwythyr!"

As he advanced toward me with the serpents on his sword spitting flames I guessed his intention. He might kill me and usurp my hunt for Twrch Trwyth, but he would never be a hunter of souls and lead them back to my cauldron, which he had one greedy eye upon.

I stared up at him savagely. "Kill me and I will hunt you mercilessly."

"This time you won't be returning from death," said Arthur triumphantly. With a backward glance at Gwythyr, "I know your secret."

So Gwythyr had utterly betrayed me as I knew he would...

When Arthur plunged his sword into my chest it was worth waiting to die to see his foiled expression when he could not find my heart.

The Song of Your Heart

'*Caer Ochran*
The Cold Castle under the stone...
Day of the king's birth'
  Meg Falconer

I felt your death-blow
before Annwn's door slammed shut
like a crash of thunder resonating across the iron grey sky.

I knew it was a death unlike any other
but still I heard the beating
of your heart.

I followed the pathways
down which your hounds had dragged
gored dragons with the membranes of their gauzy wings
 torn,
headless giants with their beards plucked out,
bleeding squealing tuskless boars,

arrived on a shore where gulls cried
of a white-prowed ship arriving like a seafarer's portent,
Arthur disembarking and three shiploads
of warriors pouring from
the hold.

I followed the trail of scorched and blackened trees
burnt down by Gwythyr's blazing sword

(trees die slowly -
their agony screamed in the back of my head).

Your spirits plucked at my sleeves and led me to the dead,
first those who had fled,
arrows protruding
from backs,
then onto the battlefield
where heads were smashed like eggshells,
severed limbs lay discarded like unwanted parcels,
and blood from hundreds of ravaging wounds reddened
 the soil
clotting slowly with the matter from spilled bowels.
I clasped my hand over my mouth.

In the distance I saw your glass fortress
which rotated in the sky at the speed of the stars
to the song of Old Mother Universe chanted by your
 bards
crash-landed on its corner like a shipwreck,
your six-thousand speechless guards
slumped on its walls
with meaningless doll-like stares.

Your spirits tugged at my hair and dragged me

to where I did not want to go with feet trailing as if stuck
 in glue
through your battered portcullis past the stairway
leading to your prison where you held
Gwythyr and his host

(imprisoning Summer so Winter rules),

Arthur's jailbreak illustrated by the sword marks
and scrapes and burns on your walls,

then into your hall where the dead lay scattered
around the epicentre of your confrontation.

I could barely look upon your body.
I could not tell if the blood drenching your furs
was that of Arthur and his warriors or yours.
I could not count your wounds for tears.
You died with a snarl and wild hair
escaping from your horned helmet.

A sword through the chest was your death:
a gaping hole through shattered ribs.
It should have pierced
your heart
but that cavern was empty as a trick birthday box.
Everyone said you were heartless,
but I knew the truth and so did
your baying hounds.

Did they know where it was hidden?

Did Creiddylad?
She who was making love with your rival
in the summer flowers?

I guess not - love is fickle.

I called to those you can trust,
those who know the scent of your sweat and blood,
to red-nosed Dormach, to Rhudd, to Gwynt,
to the red-eared, red-spotted,
red-pawed ones;

so commenced your heart's hunt.

Your hunters rode pale horses
and the long-striding giants rode none.
A dragon followed for a while circling above
then flew down and fell asleep
with a cave-like yawn.

As we galloped through burnt-out forests
and empty plains raided of cattle
and the furious tides crashed
beneath screaming gulls

I noticed the otherlight dimming,
the remaining colour washing out of the green hills

leaving everything dishwater grey then
darkening to the grey of ash.

My companions were fading.
I who journeyed here in soul faded too.
Your death was the death of the soul-world –
the death of all souls.

The magic of your world was running out...

Your hounds dug wildly beneath trees,
bloodying their frantic paws
to find only the hearts of
dead badgers,

sniffed suspiciously at the edge of pools
where I searched through reeds
as if looking for a baby
in the bulrushes,
plunged in
and emerged draped in duck-weed.

We snatched a still-beating heart
from a bear's claws (not yours).

We searched every cave for a heart-shaped box.
When we found one
and the keys to the lock

inside was only a locket and a love letter in an illegible
 hand.
When we had searched everywhere in Annwn
we rode across Thisworld following
your fading heart beat.

We found your heart in the unlikeliest of places.

Clutching it tightly, fearing every time it skipped a beat,
we galloped back to Annwn with our hearts
beating just as wildly.

Through the fortresses within fortresses
through secret tunnels
and hidden doors
we bore your body
from Caer Pedryvan,
Caer Vedwit, Caer Rigor,
Caer Vandwy, Caer Golud,
to Caer Ochran: the cold castle under the stone.

Into your empty chest we placed your still-beating heart.

The life returned to your limbs.
Your wounds closed like theatre curtains.
The otherlight returned to your eyes illuminating all of
 Annwn.
Putting your hand to your heart as if remembering

something forgotten you sat up and smiled one of your
rare smiles.
The hills greened and new saplings shot up.
I heard the distant lowing of cattle.

Your fortresses within fortresses
began to turn like the polyhedron
you showed me floating in the air
when I was young.

I stood in the sacred centre on the day of your birth
and sung the Song of Your Heart
with all my heart

and so my bardic prayer will continue
until the end of the world.

Leader of the Hunt II

'Arthur summoned Gwyn son of Nudd to him, and asked him if he knew anything about Twrch Trwyth. He said that he did not'
  Culhwch and Olwen

As I slept my sleep of recovery Arthur usurped my leadership of the hunt.

I was awoken by huntsmen skewered on tusks, hounds thrown like rags onto sodden soil, bloody-nostriled horses thrashing their death-throes.

My traitorous heart cared for them.

I called to my spirits, "Take it and hide it. Tell nobody where it is, not even me."

I went to Eire where Twrch Trwyth and his seven piglets had rumpled up the land with their spade-like snouts, turned over the hills, trampled decimation through towns and markets. It reminded me of the day the ancient chieftain first put on silver bristles and rampaged across Prydain possessed by the fury of the spirits of Annwn.

I had not known what he was, and doubted Arthur knew, as he fought against Twrch Trwyth for nine nights and days killing only one piglet.

Arthur and his huntsmen did not realise I hunted them, gathering the souls of tusk-torn men, horses, and hounds, adding them to my hunt.

Already I could see his leashes were slipping.

Twrch Trwyth and his piglets returned to Prydain across the sea, legs pumping in an orgy of sea-foam, pulling every ship into their deadly wake. In Daugleddyf they consumed man and beast with omnivorous teeth. They stood at bay in Cwm Cerwyn and Glyn Nyfer, painting the woodlands red with the blood of Arthur's huntsmen. Corpses floated on the tides of Arthur's foolishness at Aber Tywi.

When Twrch Trwyth was wounded in Glyn Ystun by Arthur's spear I opened a shadowy passageway and drove him into Annwn's dens.

The hounds yapped and Arthur's men beat the undergrowth to no avail.

"Gwyn ap Nudd."

Arthur thought he could summon me.

My laughter rocked the boughs as I appeared from where I already stood with antlers grazing the skies and notched an arrow with his name on it.

"Do you know anything about Twrch Trwyth?"

"I know nothing," I shook my head.

The trees shook with me shedding beech mast and acorns to accentuate my lie.

"Where he is? What he is? Who...?"

Too well I recalled my battle against the mighty boar and his slipping through countless forms as his fury drained out with his blood until I held a dead man. I'd taken him home to his family to be buried in a stony tomb with his comb, shears, and razor between his ears as a reminder of his human identity to keep his boar-bristles at bay.

His soul had refused to return with me.

"I know nothing."

I disappeared into the shadows between the boughs.

Arthur shook his fist and demanded the slaughter of Twrch Trwyth's piglets, who died like fallen stars on the mountains and in the valleys of Prydain, names seeping into the land like decaying flesh.

(Their names remain, obdurate as skulls, with the names of their hunters.)

Twrch Trwyth leapt to avenge his piglets. In the Hafren his comb, shears, and razor were stolen, then he escaped into the Cornish sea.

As I predicted, Arthur dared not mount my water-horse, Du y Moroedd, with his hull-like chest, oars for legs, and slippery jellyfish heart. As I took the reins my hounds broke their leashes and barked across the waves to where I embraced my old foe until his fury bled out.

Once again I laid Twrch Trwyth in his tomb. His soul refused to return and I cursed my mistake which has bound us in this chase forever.

"Gwyn ap Nudd."

The next time Arthur summoned me he was lost in the mist in the northern uplands. Gwythyr rode beside him. Behind was a procession of warriors; Caw leading a mule carrying two huge glass bottles, four servants, the last struggling bent-backed lugging my cauldron.

I knew where he was heading and why; with increasing frequency I dreamt of the death of Orddu, 'Very Black,' daughter of Orwen, 'Very White,' the last of my Inspired Ones, custodians of my sacred valley.

I appeared where the path forked aboard a stallion of mist. "The left fork will lead to the place you call Pennant Gofid in the uplands of Hell."

For three nights and days they rode into deeper terrors. Glimpses of the accusing faces of giants in the crags, the hollow faces of dead warriors, wraiths of fog who took their guises bearing portents of their gruesome ends robbed them of their nerve, their wits, their minds.

Some fell by sheer accident, others attempting to flee. With a prayer to God one leapt and is still suspended between Hell and Heaven.

I stalked them with my hounds, picking them off one by one, before a slip of the mist revealed the entrance to the valley.

I will never forget how somewhere my heart swelled with pride when I saw Orddu standing defiant in the cave entrance, black-robed, black-haired, black-faced, flexing her talons, or how my whisper encouraging Arthur to send his servants in and their battered return triggered his loss of temper and the knife-blow that sliced her in twain.

As I held Orddu's spirit whilst Arthur drained the blood from her veins I knew she would never be whole until the last drop was returned.

A flash of lightning over the nine towers of Ysbaddaden Bencawr announced his beheading. I entered his hall after the final revellers had departed from the wedding of Culhwch and Olwen. My empty cauldron stood in the centre.

Gwlgad's horn and Llwyr's cup had run dry. Gwyddno's hamper lay kicked over. Teirtu's harp played a sad song.

Ysbaddaden's headless trunk sprawled across his cliff-high table. His emasculated head was on a stake. Not only had his brittle hawthorn-bush beard been shaved with Twrch Trwyth's equipment, but the barber had pared his flesh down to the bone and sliced off both his ears.

Seeing his beard heaped in the corner with Gwyddolwyn's bottles, I realised the magical shaving lotion was Orddu's blood. My pulse thundered in my ears as I thought of her, the last of her lineage, her life's essence, which could change the fate of worlds, used for... this...

A pink thread of twitching muscle revealed Ysbaddaden's soul still resided in his head. "Ysbaddaden Bencawr!" I turned on him furiously.

Without the men with forks he could not raise his heavy eyelids. "Gwyn?" he mumbled.

"You have betrayed the names of your kindred, my huntsmen and hounds, the witches of Annwn."

"I didn't... didn't... mean... for th... th..."

"No, but if you had allowed Olwen to take a husband centuries ago, Arthur would not have twisted your 'impossible' tasks into an excuse for massacring your kindred and you wouldn't have died so barbarously."

Ysbaddaden's mouth drooped and saliva trickled from its corner.

"So what's it to be?" I asked him. "Are you going to return to Annwn and face your kin or would you rather live on in this earless old head?"

"Bury me with it," drooled Ysbaddaden, "beneath... beneath this fortress. Never... never... never let my nine towers be found again."

As I buried the Head of Giants in the centre of his courtyard, the gatekeepers returned and the mastiffs howled for him. I wove enchantments around his northern hills and surrounded them with mist.

The fury of headless, beardless giants; cloven-headed witches; huntsmen, horses, hounds, swept through me tempting me with its unleashing upon Arthur's fortresses and villainous warriors.

I held them firmly on the battlefields of Annwn.

"The day will come," I reassured them, "when Arthur meets his end."

The Huntsman and the Water Horse

'No steed will be of any use to Gwyn in hunting... except Du'
Culhwch and Olwen

I.

"Huntsman, will you ride with me
beyond the rumours of this town
where the old port-mote once met
and soundless ships sunk down?

"Huntsman, will you ride with me
where burning tides sear the shore
and breakwater fills my fetlocks
with the yearning I see in your soul?

"Huntsman, will you ride with me
to seek the prey you long for
where seas are deep as your desire
and hoofbeats outrun your hunger?"

II.

"Old horse, I'd like to ride with you.
But don't you remember my name?

How we met on this tideless brink
and I learnt your treacherous ways?

"Old horse, I'd like to ride with you.
But don't you remember the time
we hurtled down to skeletal depths
and you learnt your world was mine?

"Old horse, I'd like to ride with you.
But don't you remember the bond
we sealed in the halls of Annwn?
How it brings you to this dock?"

III.

"By Annwn, I remember you.
Your name is Gwyn ap Nudd.
Hunter of souls from the deep
will you ride with me?"

"Across the blackest ocean
from this world's birth to its end
to seek the prey we were born to seek
I will ride with you, old friend."

Arthur Refuses to Die

'And in that bed there li'th a knight
his woundes bleeding day and night.
At that bed's foot there li'th a hound
licking the blood as it runs down'
  Corpus Christi Carol

A battlefield is a poor choice of bed
for a king, a knight, or pauper.
Armour grates like rusted springs.
There is no soft pillow for the head,
no goosedown cover but the cloak
of an enemy with a glittering knife
in his belly. The croak of ravens
is the only lullaby for bed-partners
sinking slowly into the long dark night.
And in that bed there li'th a knight

who I hunted across a dozen battlefields
gathering the souls of his comrades
from beneath lacerated shields.
Amidst the detritus I find him lying
with a dozen bloody fissures in his mail
and wound in his side half a foot wide.
He breathes through its gaping flaps
and not through the pale cold lips

by which he defies me, refusing to die,
his woundes bleeding day and night.

I recite the names of all he slaughtered.
He will not look into my eyes where
they are gathered shaking their spears.
He clutches his soul like a bear cub
and refuses childishly to give it back.
We tussle with it like dogs over a bone.
We tug-of war and it stretches like rope
and hisses snake-like as he prays to God.
I warn him of a stony bed underground:
"At that bed's foot there li'th a hound

who will never leave your bedside.
All the magic of Morgana - healing water,
poultices of comfrey, camomile, calendula,
the charms and spells she incants with her
iron cauldron and black feather wand
will never heal your death-wound.
The bleeding will never stanch.
As you toss and turn in your dreams
of Empire I will wait as a patient hound
licking the blood as it runs down."

IV.
The Fall of
the North

The Brightness Beyond Endurance

'I saw a brightness too great for human senses to endure. I saw, too, numberless martial battalions in the heaven, like flashing lightning, holding in their hands fiery lances and glittering spears which they shook most fiercely at me. So I was torn out of myself and an evil spirit seized me and assigned me to the wild things of the woods, as you see'
The Life of St Kentigern

Gwenddydd trod lightly through the brightness. Her hands were full of butterflies. Yellow-faced siskins chattered in the pine canopy; they were the sunlight, bright as day, loud as splinters of light. The taut limbs of her soul slowly stretched like a wild cat into a sigh. *So this is the place where I shall meet my brother again...*

Her mind ran back to the pitter-patter of two pairs of dirty-soled feet, the identical feet of twins in shapeless smocks: she and Myrddin running on pine needles in the tracks of boar and deer, chasing the tails of squirrels, trying to close their hands on darters and dragonflies.

Following a trail of wood ants back to their mound-like fortress (nearly as tall as Caer Gwenddolau!). Disappearing into a tunnel with the spindly-legged, shiny-backed soldiers. Darkness, warmth, clambering over each other, feeling the way with sensuous antennae. Snapping back to see the same sense of wonder in Myrddin's pine-green eyes.

They'd shared visions, dreams, their ability to communicate with the wild creatures of Celyddon until they came of age; Myrddin joined Gwenddolau's cattle-raiding warriors and Gwenddydd married a Christian warlord.

Longing to forget the grey days of her marriage, pallid as bed sheets, circumscribed by a golden ring, Gwenddydd returned to the forest of her youth, listening to the tap-tap-tap of a woodpecker, glimpsing his red head and green wings, pointing him out to her brother.

Together they stumbled through leafy clumps of blaeberry and cowberry, made hummocks of glittering wood moss their thrones, played king and queen then cast down their crowns. Tracing the runners of creeping ladies tresses, fingering skirt-like flowers on long stems, Gwenddydd noted they looked nothing like a lady's hair. If only she'd been born a wild plant and not a lady.

A snorting and grunting; the trees stood aside. Gwenddydd and Myrddin gripped each other in fear and glee as a stripy pack of wild boar piglets rumpused into the glade, runneling up the mud with hard snouts, digging a mess, kicking and squealing. Then after them a sow laboured her big belly into view with milk dripping from her laden udders.

Myrddin had loved those little piglets, offered them truffles and composed them poems. They'd loved and trusted him unconditionally even when he returned to where they snuffled beneath roots with guilt and battle-madness stamped on his hollow face.

If only they had stayed in the forest and he had not succumbed to the drums of war, carnxyes squealing like stuck pigs. If it wasn't for warlords, mead, riches, and the cursed bards singing up fool's gold promises of immortality.

Gwenddydd remembered that hall. She and Myrddin sneaking from their pallets to peer through a crack in the door. The blazing fire beneath the cauldron and the smell of roasting bull. Gwenddolau, massive in bull-horns and a bull-skin; a great, steaming, stomping bull of a man devouring the Bull God, Tarw.

Gwenddydd remembered the bull sacrifice. Brown Mawr, the prime bull of the herd, strong-horned, slab-shouldered, boisterous, virile, walking to the pit like a lamb. Gwenddolau's knife slitting his throat, his blood pouring into the pit to feed the war-gods whilst grown men wept.

As the warriors partook of the bull-meat, the flesh of the Bull God, and passed round the mead-horn, in the heat of the flames they were transformed. Husbands, sons, men who herded cows and kissed women, were consumed by battle-lust. Their eyes blazed with the fire's crimson light. As Gwenddolau's bard stepped forward to sing of blood-drenched spears and rolling heads, they grew horns, their shoulders broadened, smoke blew from their nostrils.

When the bard sung of Gwyn ap Nudd, fierce Bull of Battle, gathering the souls of the dead, Gwenddydd was left cold by a vision; mute, trembling with her ashen twin until their mother scooped them up.

Gwenddydd had begged Myrddin not to get caught up in the daring-do of Gwenddolau's hall. She'd begged her mother and father not to force her to marry Rhydderch Hael. But fate was merciless as the pair of eagles who feasted on Gwenddolau's enemies, pecking out their eyes, clawing open their bellies, tugging their intestines to the stars.

Fate was ghastly as the Three Bull Spectres: Bull Chieftains, like Gwenddolau, but neither living nor dead, neither human nor bull, doomed to wander the world in that state forever; ghoulish as the *gwyllon* amongst whom Myrddin had wandered for ten and twenty years.

Back to the forest as the sun went down on their youth, casting its last orange beams through the smudges of pine as midges descended like crazed warriors thirsty for human blood. Gwenddydd and Myrddin hid themselves in a bower, piled up a defence of twigs and leaves, and prayed they would be safe as wood ants as night descended.

An owl hooted. Through an eye-gap they watched as by the light of the moon the trees donned faces and began to move in a root-dance, twig-like things springing from the portals of their mouths. The mounds opened, birthing antlered warriors in the skins of bears, wolves, deer.

Footsteps crashed through the forest swaying the ground like a bridge. A giant with long and hanging ears, as if they'd been pulled down in a wrestling match, hauled itself into the glade, wrapped in a pine-needle cloak, leaning on a crudely carved club.

A wolf with an exuberant white ruff and soft, deadly step walked beside it. Nose twitching, ears pricked, it turned its eyes, bright as the afterlife, toward their hiding place. Gwenddydd stared transfixed. She saw the capacity for death in its watchful gaze, but that night it walked away.

Gwenddydd and Myrddin were reborn from their bower at dawn to the melody of a song thrush, layer upon layer of pink and yellow sound, as chaffinch, siskin, gold-crest, joined the dawn chorus. How they'd laughed and danced, twiggy-haired, dirty-footed, grubby-kneed, unknowing that time in the forest was their last.

Gwenddydd had thought she could survive anything after the terrors of that dark, mysterious night. She'd never guessed how her marriage would wear her down; the sounds and colours of the forest fading from her until she was pale and emotionless as a wrung-out bath towel.

The only thing that had kept her sane was her two beautiful children, Derwyn and Tanwen. Derwyn reminded her so much of Myrddin, of their father, only by some miracle he did not share their seriousness nor their lust for battle and prestige. He had not wanted to fight for Rhydderch, but fighting was demanded of him by his birthright.

Gwenddydd's marriage to Rhydderch should have brought an end to the growing conflict between the Men of the North. But love was no remedy to the power-hunger shared by the northern warlords, turning kinsman against kinsman for land, cattle, the fatal glow of fame in the bardic halls.

In Gwenddydd's lifetime it seemed the fate of all young men was to feed the ravens; to be snatched to the realm of Gwyn. Not just Derwyn, but Tanwen too. How could she have been such a fool to don a man's armour and march to Arfderydd?

It was the curse of Christianity, the legacy of Arthur, the foolish notion one God should rule all, which drove Rhydderch to join the alliance against Gwenddolau, the last British ruler who worshipped the old gods, and forced Myrddin to fight against her son and daughter.

Once again, Gwenddydd watched paralysed through Myrddin's eyes as Gwenddolau lay dead by Derwyn's hand, bleeding out like a slaughtered bull. Myrddin had loved the Bull-Protector of Arfderydd, who treated him like a son when their father died, made him his prime warrior, beguzzled him with mead, gifted him a golden torque.

When Gwenddolau died on Derwyn's spear, Myrddin's world fell apart. Loss unravelled him. Lust for vengeance burnt in his blood. He failed to recognise Derwyn through the crimson screen.

Myrddin attacked Gwenddolau's killer with an apocalyptic bellow. Oblivious to his opponent's blows, he hacked him down, turned on the slender warrior fighting beside him, the next and the next, until, surrounded by corpses, he collapsed from his battle-wounds.

When Myrddin gained consciousness he met the staring pine-green eyes of a woman with strands of tawny hair shaken loose from her helmet. Recognising her, "Gwenddydd!" he forced himself onto his hands and knees, a whimper rising in his throat, crawled closer.

No, but a young woman who bore a striking resemblance to her. He knew in his soul she was kin: Gwenddydd's daughter. And who was that, near Gwenddolau's corpse, staring at him with a single eye like his own, like his father's, the other sealed shut by blood? Gwenddydd's son.

Grief and self-loathing welled within Myrddin. He howled in desolation. Rain poured down, flooding the battlefield. Ravens glutted themselves on corpses. Myrddin longed for death to erase his torment, his guilt. He slipped and slithered in the mud, groaning in anguish, his desperate hand searching for a blade, any blade, to end his misery.

Thunder rolled overhead. The battlefield was flooded by unendurable brightness. When Myrddin looked up, the light bedazzled and burnt his eyes. In the midst of its searing he saw the flashing images of warriors with fiery lances and glittering spears. He saw his father! And then a shape, a form, a bull-horned figure, who seemed composed of battalions of the dead.

At a single gesture of his hand, the warriors descended to gather the souls from the corpses, pulling them out like spider-silk to stand pale, shining, lightning-like beside their bodies. How beautiful they were in death, Derwyn and Tanwen, a handsome young man, a bold young woman. How easily they went into the arms of Myrddin's father.

"Take me, take me!" he begged.

The terrible figure in the skies lowered his gaze to Myrddin. Myrddin felt the life ebb from his limbs. A spirit gripped his shoulder and tore him out of himself. Instead of taking him back to his kindred, into the arms of the Gatherer of Souls, it pulled him away from the battlefield over the hills and moors to the forest of Celyddon.

Gwenddydd recalled the first time she witnessed this vision. It recurred as she lay on her sick bed, locked in her bedroom so Rhydderch's court would not find out about her madness. At first she'd hated her brother with an intensity that vanquished all those years of love, with the sharpness of an assassin's blade, with the venom of all the snakes of Celyddon. She'd cursed Myrddin, wished him dead. If she'd had a knife to cut the sutures connecting them in vision she would have severed them many times, but she had not. Gwenddydd and her twin were bound in endurance together.

As if watching through gaps in clouds, Gwenddydd caught glimpses of her brother. Firstly he was perched, bird-like, gibbering in the branches of a tree, flinching at each gust of wind, tucking his head beneath his wings.

After many seasons had passed, he shimmied down squirrel-like, slowly regained his appetite, feeding on nuts and berries, roots, leaves, strips of bark, insects. When snow lay so thick it covered his thighs and his beard was laced with icicles, the wolf with the lambent eyes lent its warmth and shared his shivering and scrawny flanks.

From the creatures of Celyddon Myrddin regained the power of speech. It came like the sap in spring; first a slow stirring at the earliest hint of warmth, then a bubbling upward, then a surge, then a flood: an unstoppable fountain.

Chwyfleian, a brook sprite, had a name for it: Awen. Myrddin's words flowed from the living waters which welled from deep beneath the earth, bearing gifts of wisdom from Annwn.

To birch and pine, hazel and apple-tree, the little piglets and the wolf, Myrddin began to speak poems and prophecies. When she heard them, they tugged at Gwenddydd's soul, for he spoke of dreams she had forgotten how to remember, imprisoned in Rhydderch's fortress. Her dreaming returned with all its childhood vivacity.

Finally, Myrddin left the forest and took to prophesying from the stone above Molendinar Burn near the chapel where Kentigern, Rhydderch's bishop, held his sermons. Kentigern complained, "Your brother has returned again to interrupt my words with his depraved ranting about future catastrophes. His words are disturbing my congregation, putting into question their faith in God.

"He has the lunacy to suggest that, even with God's will, we Britons will not triumph against the Anglo-Saxons. That more men will run mad in Celyddon. That the Kingdoms of Gododdin, Rheged, Elmet, and even Alt Clut will eventually fall! That the following centuries will be wracked by further wars where men fight with lightning and fly like birds of thunder bringing deadly storms."

Gwenddydd recognised the fragments of her dreams and was certain they came from the Awen. They were warnings about future bloodshed, the fall of the North because its rulers were so busy fighting amongst themselves. Endless wars without and within. No end to the deaths of the young, the poor fallen skylarks who were dispensable as pieces on a gwyddbwyll board to the heartless warlords.

Gwenddydd wanted to go to Myrddin, but her time on her sick bed had left her legs unsteady, her pulse weak. Her head spun whenever she stood. One spring morning, as the blackbirds sang, she determined to leave or die trying. She pushed herself into a sitting position, slowly moved one leg out of the bed, then the other, pressed the soles of her feet flat onto the straw. She took a deep breath, prepared to push herself up with both hands.

The door swung open. It was Rhydderch, tall and regal in his armour, accompanied by Kentigern in his bishop's smock.

Their eyes widened when they saw Gwenddydd halfway out of bed. Rhydderch whispered something to Kentigern. The bishop shook his head. "She must know."

Fear gripped Gwenddydd: an urgent fear like a cold fish swimming in the depths of her belly.

"Your brother came to the stone above Molendinar Burn today," Kentigern spoke gravely. "I am afraid he has fallen deeper into insanity for he prophesied his own death."

The fish in Gwenddydd's belly sank like a stone.

"He said he was destined to be stoned, then fled back to the forest. To test whether he prophesied truly, I sent a courier to ask again how he would die. His second reply was that he would be pierced by a stake. To ascertain his madness, I sent a different courier, who returned with the reply he would drown. Even if his prophesies are not true, he is evidently in extreme distress; in such states many men have been known to end their lives advertently or inadvertently.

"It is my duty to God to ensure he receives the sacrament before his death, for he has been possessed by an evil spirit. The hold of the Devil must be broken so his soul can depart to Heaven. Therefore I need to know whether you have glimpsed his whereabouts."

Each of Kentigern's words jarred Gwenddydd. Living within the restrictions of Christianity had cut her off from the forest, its spirits, from her ancestors, and from Gwyn ap Nudd to whom her soul and her brother's should truly return. Myrddin's subjection to the sacrament was the worst thing she could imagine.

"I won't tell you," she said, "his soul does not belong to your God."

"She is possessed," said Kentigern to Rhydderch.

Rhydderch stared at his wife in anguish.

Gwenddydd realised she couldn't live this faded existence anymore. *They think I'm possessed, then let me be possessed!* She called on the spirits of Annwn for strength. A blast of wind rushed in, as if released directly from the mouth of the Otherworld, throwing Rhydderch and Kentigern against the wall.

Horned, beaked, winged figures surrounded Gwenddydd and tore her out of herself. She was lifted through the window, leaving Rhydderch's fortress, Dumbarton Rock, the river Clutha, flying north to Celyddon. She landed in the branches of a pine in the form of a tawny hawk, ran as pine marten, wild cat, lynx, hunting for her brother.

By the time Gwenddydd found Myrddin it was too late. As prophesied he lay drowned in the shallows of the river Tweed, pierced by a stake, bony limbs stoned black and blue. His mouth gulped open. His wild hair flowed with reeds amongst stones and fishes. Yet the expression in his pearly eyes spoke of something beyond the pain of death.

The air around Gwenddydd rippled. Like a shining water sprite Myrddin appeared to stand beside her. She looked at his face, resolved of battle-madness, filled with the wonder of the forest, but older, wiser, irreparably sad. "I'm sorry," Myrddin spoke from turbulent depths.

Tears drenched Gwenddydd's face as she thought of Derwyn and Tanwen, springing from the wells of Awen that her family shared. Yet her rage against her brother was gone. "I forgive you," Gwenddydd said.

For a moment the sadness left Myrddin's eyes and he smiled.

"Although I do not forgive Arthur, Gwenddolau, Rhydderch," Gwenddydd continued, "the warlords of the past, present, and future who haunt our dreams."

"Then share your dreams whilst you can," said Myrddin. "I will dream with you and be waiting in the brightness beyond endurance; the forest of our youth."

Myrddin's Scribe

We hold the inner space for God above:
clear, calm, silent, only to hear him galloping
in like a forest: thunder of deer-storm,
cacophony of boar-grunt bristled as pine.
Naked and skinny he takes his throne:
a steep stone beside Molendinar Burn.

Though he lives off only common air,
his words are juicy berries,
succulent apples, cracking hazelnuts
whose wisdom only chewing can divine.
Some have horns and antlers. Some are stags
alive with rude desire. Some have swinging udders.
Some have feathers and fluttering heart-beats
racing between sky and heaven.

My heart stutters and leaps when Kentigern
commands me to take quill and vellum,
with a shaking, itinerant hand pen
huge, outrageous monsters
taking me on shaggy backs
with clip-clop of trotters to dance goat-foot
in a glade or suckle swine. An old boar
runs at me with curved tusks.
Suddenly I'm helpless; lying bleeding, gored,

on the forest floor as fur-coated warriors
step forward with stumps of spears,
twisted shields, jagged swords.
Each bears a death story:
a severed limb, broken head, belly gouged.
They do not stop arriving from Celyddon's darkness
in charred pieces ranting about fiery skies,
falling through everlasting night,
white-light, lightning soldiers,
filling my head with catastrophic pain
and unending war until I scream, "No more!"
I want to turn back to the forest. Run back
to the wild creatures but see we've gone too far
unless some prophecy can stop it.

I dip my quill in the ink,
pen these roaring and bloody words
coursing through my veins marking stiff spears
and gaping wounds. A madman's agony soothed only
by sketches of leafy foliage, the smile
of a dog, the face of a bear.

My last life seeps into the vellum,
snatched away by Kentigern.
Disliking what he sees,
he throws it into Molendinar Burn.

In my dark cell I die slowly,
taking hope in Myrddin's words:

his prophecies will be inscribed again
in a sea-town of the Cymry. Fierce animal
portraits and green branching letters
will be inscribed again and again
until we learn to love the forest
and turn from war.

Severed Head

I hold a severed head.
The flesh is old, grey, leathery,
from hundreds of years in a peat bog.
Dark tufts of hair remain like grass.
Its eyes have been swallowed.

"Whose is it?" You place
your hands on mine moving them
over the skull like a phrenologist
reading a war-torn childhood
and lust for love and power.

You ask if I feel the burning
of the soul when I touch the crown.
There is no heat, but the cold thrum
of an old and watchful presence
tingles up my finger bones.

You speak of apotropaic magic -
how a head buried on a boundary
defends its kingdom until dug up
it turns inwards to work curses
with dried-out withered lips.

When the mouth does not move
you tell me to "listen" and open

my inner ear like a creaking door
to an unfamiliar tongue rousing
images of halls of praise-songs,

treacherous whispers becoming
chants of hatred, pennants flapping
like the wings of screaming ravens,
an assassin's knife and a cousin's
blade slicing head from neck.

"Whose head is it? Who sings?"
My mouth will not form the dry words.
Forgetting your touch my grey fingers
scrabble through the ghostly air
clutching the hair of nothing.

The Shield of Rheged

I.

'There were three rauens sat on a tree,
They were as blacke as they might be.
With a downe, derrie, derrie, derrie down'
  The Three Ravens

Who comes next to hear the tale of a one-legged raven? Are you hungry for battle-ravens in the skies? The ravens of Urien Rheged? Ravens croaking over gore as Gwyn ap Nudd gathers the souls of the warriors of the fallen North? Do you want to know how I lost my leg?

My words once cost an eye, my son, but now I'll settle for a lock of your long, manly hair to weave into my nest to which my beloved will never return. She is dead and, like the Gatherer of Souls, I live on.

Beautiful, beautiful, black as the locks of your Moorish forefathers, black as a raven, black as the ever-beating heart of war...

I'll begin with three ravens on the Shield of Rheged. I was the oldest of three black-winged sons. How old? What came first, the ravens or the shield? It's difficult to remember after so many blows to the head...

But the story goes that I was one of three ravens who sat on the tree beside Rhyd y Gyfarthfa where the wild dogs gather to bark. We have always hunted together, ravens leading wolves or dogs to easy prey, wolves or dogs tearing corpses apart for ravens.

Yet it wasn't carrion that called us to Rhyd y Gyfarthfa. It was a fateful event. And all fateful events need barking dogs and croaking ravens, preferably three ravens sitting on a tree.

Modron, Daughter of Afallach, was washing at the ford. And what was she washing? Well, it wasn't her hair or her apple-green limbs, my son, although her pink-blushed bosoms were a sight to behold. No! She was washing ripped and bloody garments of Rheged's immortal blue. Kneading and soaping, kneading and soaping, and as she kneaded and soaped she wailed:

Woe to the Kings of Rheged!
Woe to the North!
Woe to Prydain!

We croaked and the dogs barked as over the horizon rode Urien on a yellow horse, fully armoured, blue cloak flowing behind him, sword in his hand, the Shield of Rheged at his thigh... the Shield of Rheged... damn!

I was supposed to tell you how we ravens got on that shield first. See what I mean about too many blows to the head? If a Saxon with white-washed hair shows his tonsils with his war-cry then slams the hilt of his forty-pound sword into your skull, time starts to bend a bit, warp, like when a weapon's first forged. Like a serpent biting its tail.

At Rhyd y Gyfarthfa many years before Urien, Ceneu son of Coel Hen (yes, Old King Cole, the Merry Old Soul, although I can tell you now he was never merry, the grumpy old git) met Modron whilst she was washing. Washing her apple-green bosoms. He fell to one knee and begged for her hand in marriage. She took him into the river, which foamed like the froth from the very first bite of an apple: piquant, sweet, refreshing, and made him King of Rheged.

That was another of those fateful events where the dogs barked and three ravens sitting on a tree croaked. And because of that Ceneu asked a blacksmith to make him a shield. Who? Well, you might have guessed, only one could meld the fates of three ravens to a shield: Gofannon of course, the forger of Caledfwlch, although that's another example of the warping of time...

Gofannon hit me on the head with his hammer. I can't remember if it was before or after he made the shield. I can still hear the ringing of his forge and the singing of the birds of Rhiannon (who stop time). Spinning round and round I can still see their circling yellow beaks and yellow eyes.

Speaking of circles, I'd best get back to Rhyd y Gyfarthfa, Modron, and the Kings of Rheged. Ceneu, Gwrwst, Meirchion, Cynfarch, all dropped to one knee before Modron, kissed her apple-sweet lips, received her blessings like windfall apples upon their kingship.

But Urien was different. With his head in the clouds of the Christian God, the thunder of the patriarchs in his ears, he did not see a goddess, but just a woman washing. He silenced the barking dogs by slitting their throats. He silenced my croaking by hitting me on the head with the same damned shield I'm enamelled on; bone-white with me, Llygaid Du, on the top left, Clustiau Du on the top right, and Big Du on the bottom. No wonder time went awry for Urien!

Needless to say, I don't remember a thing after that, just the ringing in my ears, a white mist-like haze and three circling ravens. When I came to, the ford was red and I was surrounded by dead dogs. Modron's skin was bruised like an apple's and she was weeping tears of blood.

The Shield will break!
The Kingdom of Rheged will fall!
My lands are broken and I am with child!

It's one of those... what do you call them? Temporal paradoxes? The question of whether Modron's rape caused Urien's death. For if it did, how could she have been washing his grave-clothes before he seized her and had his way with her? Did she foresee her fate, reach through the wormholes of time to guide the hand of his assassin, snatch his blood-stained garments and drag them back to set his fate as revenge? Only the serpents know and Modron. I wouldn't recommend asking her about it, she hit me on the head and... you don't want to hear about any more blows to the head, but how I lost my leg? Alright, alright, your hair is beautiful...

II.

'A head I bear by my side,
The head of Urien, the mild leader of his army -
And on his white bosom the sable raven is perched'
  The Death of Urien

We'll have to circle to Urien's assassination, another of those fateful events. Beforehand, Urien had united the kingdoms of the North and made a good few enemies. Gwallog ap Lleenog, Brân ap Ywerydd, and Morgan Fwlch paid Urien lip-service whilst plotting his end. They joined his campaign against Theodoric's Angles on Ynys Metcaut.

My brothers and I followed, hungry as always for carrion and glittering rings and golden torques to add to our hoards. Drunk on blood as warriors on mead, giddy on the songs of bloody-browed bards, we never thought of finding mates or claiming territories!

Perhaps it was the blood (or the eyes - rubbery as hard-boiled eggs and soft in the middle - splendid!) that did it on Ynys Metcaut when I failed to notice Theodoric's angry roar, the swing of his battle-axe. The blades of that axe were huge as crescent moons. It weighed a hundred pounds and could have felled a minotaur. Theodric hit me on the head and... alright, alright, I'm getting to it!

Then, he chopped off my leg. I came to in agony, bleeding to death, in the middle of a hurricane as Gwyn ap Nudd gathered the souls of the dead (when Gwyn hits you on the head you really are a goner). My life flashed before me: a medley of swords and staggering dead men. I turned away from the bright, burning eye of the storm and asked for a chance to love. Gwyn agreed, but on one condition: that I leave the Shield of Rheged and join his ravens.

So I left the shield and that's why it broke. Others will claim it was shattered by Theodric's battle-axe, but that does not explain the missing raven from the top left, his only remnant a black clawed leg. I guess you're wondering what happened to my brothers. They lived on to fight for Owain (yes, the son of Urien and Modron). They died and were buried with Owain and the remains of the shield. But time is getting ahead of itself again like Morgan's chariot. It took him to any destination as quickly as he wished; that's how his assassin got away so fast!

Alright, I'm cronking on again... back to Ynys Metcaut and my leg. It was a goner, poor thing, by the time my beloved came with her atom-black eyes and storm black feathers, took me in her talons to her treetop roost. Above the pounding waves she stanched my bleeding with mosses, bandaged my stump with ribbons stripped from the garments of the dead. Her black beak brushed mine as she nourished me back to health on entrails and fleshy morsels from the battlefield (she kept the eyes for herself, greedy thing!).

Urien's army fought against Theodric's for three nights and three days and triumphed. Theodric fell with a minotaur's roar and his battle-axe nearly cleft the island in two. It's said his death-god came for him, but that was none of my business; I was now on Gwyn's orders.

My first order came after Urien and his army sailed back from Ynys Metcaut and set up camp at Aber Lleu. At dawn, before the cock cried, a cry of woe, "Urien is dead!" echoed through the unhitching tents, "by the murderous hand of an assassin! Search every tent, every village!"

Every dead king needs a sable raven to glut upon his breast, to unpick the sinews of his soul, undo his lordship, for in the lands of the dead there is no king but Gwyn, and all souls are one.

That raven was me. When they laid Urien out in grave-clothes of Rheged's finest blue with the remains of the shield, I took his eyes, blue as a juvenile raven's, pecked at his wound. That assassin's knife was expertly slid between Urien's ribs into his heart without risk of outcry. Llofan Llawddifro was never caught, but he met his raven.

As the men of Rheged mourned and flew black flags, fluttering like raven's wings, Gwallog, Brân, Morgan, and their armies turned against them. The camp became a battlefield as I loosened Urien's soul from his corpse. Rising, he stared appalled into my black eyes.

"What? Don't say you were expecting angels? Is this not an honour, your death-rites performed by the oldest raven on your shield? Don't look at me as if I'm a stranger. I've been watching you since birth. I've seen everything except your rape of Modron and that was only because you hit me on the head."

Urien looked like he wanted to hit me again, but his hands could not grasp his sword. His arms flapped uselessly as he surveyed the battle-scene. From the camp: a heave of ragged canvases and spears, rode Llywarch, Urien's cousin, sword in hand, his enemies behind him.

"They're coming for your head!" I warned Urien. "Good job I got those eyes whilst I had the chance..."

In one deft sweep, Llywarch cut off Urien's head and grasped it by the hair. Sheathing his sword, he threw the broken pieces of the Shield of Rheged into his saddlebag, then spurred his horse into a gallop.

"At least your cousin has it, for now..."

"My head, my shield, my kingdom," Urien croaked. Good, he was gaining feathers.

"We can't stay long, unless you wish to become an angry ghost."

"Where are we going?"

"To the Table of the Stars. But first, we must find out how you can make amends to Modron."

I can't tell you exactly what Urien had to do, but let it be said he is still very busy...

Afterward, I returned to my beloved and that spring we made our first nest; lined with twigs, rags from the banners of Rheged, and the hair of dead warriors. She laid five blue-grey eggs, the colour of the stone Urien was buried beneath. Our three sons and two daughters grew strong and healthy on the spoils of war. We hatched many broods as Rheged fell, the shield was buried, and Angle and Saxon triumphed.

I glutted on the breasts of Gwallog, Brân, and Morgan. (I didn't tell you the rhyme about how Gwallog lost his eye, did I? Some say it was plucked out by an accursed tree, others by a corpse-goose: a raven).

Sadly, my beloved aged. Her feathers faded with the storm in her eyes. By the Battle of Catraeth she was too weak to fly. When I returned from the battlefield, mouth and claw filled with carrion, she was empty and feather-light. I have never known such grief as when I committed her soul to the hurricane. Gwyn and I had a little man-to-man talk about immortality and love for mortals; I haven't loved again.

Since then I have followed Gwyn to every place the warriors of Prydain have fought and been lain to rest: from the East to the North, to the East to the South, to the homeland of your Moorish forefathers. My beloved is dead but, like the Gatherer of Souls, I live on.

Lamentation for Catraeth

'By fighting they made women widows,
Many a mother with her tear on her eyelid'
  Y Gododdin

After Catraeth battle flags sway in the wind.
Storm darks our hair. Our tears are rain.
We press cheeks against cold skin,
load biers with sons and husbands
who will never drink in the mead-hall again,
lift weapons, smile across a furrowed field,
mend the plough, yoke oxen, share a meal,
touch ought but blood-stained soil,
chilled fingers reticent to let go.

Storm sky breaks. Our love pours out.
Ravens descend on soft wings to take them.
How we wish they would take our burning eyes,
flesh we rend with nails unkempt
from the year they left for Din Eiddyn,
drunk their reward before it was earned

at dawn with sharpened spears
at daybreak with clashing spears
at noon with bloody spears
at dusk with broken spears
at night with fallen spears,
shattered shields and severed heads.

Seven days of wading through blood.
Of each three hundred only one lives.
Their steel was dark-blue. Now it is red.
Because of mead and battle-madness
our husbands and sons are dead.

We rend our veils. The veil is rent.
We long to tear out our hearts
and offer them instead
to the Gatherer of Souls approaching
with the ravens and hounds of death,
whose face is black as our lament,
whose hair is the death-wind,
whose touch is sorrow,
whose heart is the portal to the Otherworld.

Our men rise up to meet him.
The march of the dead is his heart-beat.
The dead of centuries march through him.
The great night is his saddle.
The dead men ride his horse.

Forefathers and foremothers hold out their hands.
We do not want to let go but they slip
through our fingers like tears
from sooty eyelids
into the eyes of others
into the eyes of their kin
to gather in the eyes of the Gatherer of Souls.

They are stars in our eyes now.
They are stars in the eyes of the hounds of death,
marching from drunken Catraeth:
the battle that knows no end.

V.
Between Sky and Air

The Fiddler

'An arrow held against the string as if it were a bow on a fiddle'
The Wildwood Tarot

I.

She dedicates her arrows of inspiration to you,
carving each from special wood,
adding feathers
plucked from the skies
before the birds knew their way back home.

She plays her bow like a fiddle.

She learnt your song from whispering tree tops,
cold winter winds, steadfast robins;
notes she strums

as her bare feet brush icy pebbles

and she tensions the strings knowing the howl
of each hound.

She has strummed at battlegrounds, gallows,
in woods where suicides hang without music.

She has followed poets across hill and moor,
sat in asylums and played your heart's chord.

She can still the notes and make silence
vibrate not to your absence
but your presence:
the holding of breath when both worlds cease

and the rain and wind stops
and hot and cold and
life and death.

II.

I stand transfixed
where bards crumble to dust

realising you are behind me
as the tension in
the bow
and fire
in the arrow
we will shoot together
to pierce a thousand thousand futures

steadying my hand on the words of this song.

If only I could summon her,
play this bow like
a fiddle

and this fletching was from real birds.

Iolo's Exchange

'Iolo ap Huw... in the other world he has exchanged his fiddle for a bugle, and become huntsman-in-chief to Gwyn ab Nudd'
  Celtic and Manx Folklore

What price would you pay to ne'er grow old?
To ride for'er the wild winds
that blow from the depths of Tal y Clegyr
from the hall of Annwn's King?

What price would you pay to ne'er grow old?
Your life? Your beloved? Your kin?
To ride for'er with a bugle horn
at the right of Annwn's King?

~

Iolo ap Huw was a fiddler
who loved fiddling more than life:
more than his sisters, brothers, and friends,
more than his maudlin wife.

He held his fiddle in a caress
lovingly under his chin
with supple fingers rousing her notes
to soar on his thrumming string.

Together they danced to a wild fay song
only he and she could sing,
he carrying her on slippered feet,
she carrying him on wings.

Together they danced East, North and South.
Tired of fiddling in Thisworld
Iolo went to Tal y Clegyr:
cursed cave of the Otherworld.

His fiddle shrilled a shivering note
yet he played her recklessly
as he sang farewell to Winny his wife
at home with his children three.

Together they danced through the darkness,
the echo of song and feet
calling to life swirling shadow-dancers
to dance with them through the deep.

Together they danced to a fortress
bright as a star in the sky
to where Annwn's King sat patiently
upon his throne of starlight.

In the hall they danced their final dance
like the throes of a dying flame
bringing tears to the eyes of Annwn's King
and sobs from his bright Queen.

"For a bugle I will give my all!"
the fiddler declaimed bold.
"My life, my beloved, all my kin.
I will give my very soul!"

"You soul is already mine," said Gwyn.
His voice grated sad and cold.
"Would you even give me your fiddle?"
"Of course!" Iolo bawled.

He unturned the keys and tore out the strings
that chorded her heart to his,
with his last farewell he snapped her neck
then stamped on her faithful chest.

As he tore her hair from his bow-string
the cry of something breaking
was rent from him yet he laid her remains
at the feet of Annwn's King.

"From henceforth you will ride for'er
and hunt at my right hand
as huntsman-in-chief summoning souls
with this bugle's wintry blast."

When Iolo blew the bugle-horn
its song was dark and mournful
as the empty hollows of his eyes
as the void within his soul.

Its clarion cheers the Cwn Annwn
o'er *mynydd, dyffryn,* and *bryn*
summoning souls from darkening lands
to the hall of Annwn's King.

The tales of their deaths chill to the bone.
Their shrieks of loss and fear
ride long through the skies after their flight
yet Iolo has no tears

for still he weeps for the fiddle
with whom he'll ne'er again dance
for all the love of Annwn's Queen
will not fix her broken heart.

~

What price would you pay to ne'er grow old?
To ride for'er the wild winds
that blow from the depths of Tal y Clegyr
from the hall of Annwn's King?

What price would you pay to ne'er grow old?
Your life? Your beloved? Your kin?
To ride for'er with a bugle horn
at the right of Annwn's King?

The Lady of Bernshaw Tower

'Gwyn ap Nudd... He went between sky and air'
  Peniarth MS. 132

'Immediately she felt as though she were sweeping through the trackless air, - she heard the rush of mighty wings cleaving the sky, - she thought the whole world lay at her feet, and the kingdoms of the earth moved on like a mighty pageant'
  Traditions of Lancashire

Sybil, the Lady of Bernshaw Tower, was not like the other ladies of her era. She cared little for sewing, fashionable dresses, entertaining guests at her silver dinner table, or gossip about eligible bachelors.

Instead Sybil enjoyed wandering the heather-bright windswept moors, picking the purple sprigs and tormentil, bog myrtle, marsh violet, gathering bilberries into a pouch with a soft prayer.

In summer her soul ascended with the songs of skylarks, but it was the harbingers of winter she loved best. As the wild swans returned she followed their hollering calls, so like the baying of hounds, to Eagle Crag where the world fell into Cliviger Gorge.

There she prayed to the Hunter to bear her away between sky and air. Great white wings swept her up and bore her far beyond the smallness of her tower, the village of Todmorden, the bustle of the northern towns to wilder climes where the wind out-roared all chatter.

When he set her down she never saw his face. On the summit of a mountain, across a rippling lake, between branches, she would see his white antlers and follow in the form of a doe on trembling legs to drink at streams of stars, behold unfamiliar constellations, stare wide-eyed in wonder at civilisations she could not have dreamt.

He was generous with his time, which he told her was not like her time, but more like a river which flowed into a multitude of times and places all at once. Yet, Nos Galan Gaeaf, the first night of winter, he told her sternly, was his own for gathering the souls of the dead. Sybil shivered, but did not consider the implications of his words.

She roamed as a deer, winter and summer, to the consternation of her maids who complained increasingly about the mud on the hems of her dresses, her knotted hair, the burrs between her filthy toes.

Sybil's household were troubled by her lack of desire for a husband and the way she opened her suitors' letters with a cut of her knife, threw them without a glance onto her fire, returned to her window.

The rumours about her wildness spread, drawing a determined huntsman to track her across the moors. William of Towneley Hall found Sybil singing to the skylarks beneath the midsummer sun and immediately wanted to possess and tame this wild and seemingly innocent creature.

When he approached she was polite, demure, unswayed by his handsomeness, the breeding of his horse. She ruffled the heads of his hounds, tickled their bellies (he was astounded by their playfulness) and asked if he preferred the rosy-pink flowers of bog rosemary to the purple-pink of bell heather and whether he could hear the grasshopper warbler.

He gave her the answers he thought she desired and nodded along as she pointed out the patterns in the clouds and descried their meanings and consequently spoke more to the wind than to him.

When dusk fell, bringing the time of his return, he took her hand and raised it to his lips. She rapidly snatched it back as if from the jaws of a rabid hound and fled like a rabbit into the heather.

Perturbed by how quickly Sybil disappeared, William swore he'd make her his. Yet no matter how hard he hunted he could not find her. Driven by desperation, he gathered several of his finest family heirlooms and paid a visit to Mause Helton, a witch as old as the gorge.

It was rumoured Mause was once a favourite of the Hunter who flew with him between sky and air. From him she learnt not only the qualities of plants and trees, the ways of the hunt, how to shift shape into bird and animal, but the mysteries of life and death. She abused those powers and he severed their bond, leaving her unable to die or live.

On countless occasions Sybil had received shaky knocks on her door from farmhands, stablelads, midwives, doctors, ladies and gentlemen with trembling voices and downturned gazes asking guiltily for help with removing the curses of Mause Helton.

Usually their suspicions were born out of superstitious

fears surrounding the sickness of a cow, the refusal of a foal to suckle, or a feverish baby to take the teat. Simple concoctions of herbs and the singing of charms usually worked. When they did not and she suspected Mause's work, Sybil sang to the winged spirits who flew with the Hunter and drew upon their aid, unravelling her magic.

Consequently, when she was out on the moors, Sybil often sensed she was being watched, glimpsed a malevolent shadow from the corner of her eye slipping away into a crack in the rocks or a buzzard-who-was-not-a-buzzard glaring down at her, flexing yellowy talons. Sybil knew Mause was jealous of her flying with the Hunter.

When William approached the old witch she was swift to offer advice on how 'the perfidious wench of Bernshaw Tower' might be caught.

On Nos Galan Gaeaf, Sybil was roaming as a deer from her tower over Warcock Hill, Crooker Hill, Hoof Stone Height, Wolf Stones, when she heard the baying of the hounds of Thisworld and saw William in pursuit.

Panicked, she fled, leaping toward Eagle Crag, breath pumping hard from her deep lungs and flaring in her small nostrils, long legs bearing her onward, certain the Hunter would save her.

As she approached the gorge, to her disconcertment, she saw a strange hound with a shiny-white coat and blood-red ears leading William's pack and gaining on her quicker than the rest. In spite of fearing what that meant, when she reached the crag, Sybil called to the Hunter, "Take me between sky and air!"

When no wings swept down and she realised she had been abandoned, Sybil sat back on her haunches and prepared for her final leap down into the steep gorge rather than facing her captor.

She was not quick enough. The teeth of the red-eared hound sank into the tendons of her hind-leg. As Sybil turned back to look at her attacker she saw unhoundlike eyes filled with hatred before William slipped a silken noose around her neck and its magic forced her into human form.

The following days were so unbearable that mercifully Sybil barely recalled them. William dragged her leashed into church to be married and into their wedding bed, then paraded her through the houses of the wealthy decked in fine dresses with braided hair. Most constrictive was the ring that would not pull over her prominent knuckles.

More painful than William's triumph and his half-hearted attempts to gain Sybil's affection was her feeling of betrayal by the Hunter. He'd not only left her at the crag, but sent one of his hounds to tear her down, not unto death, but to a life of domesticity creamy-white as her manicured nails, punctuated by the ring of the dinner bell.

Whilst William slept Sybil wept into her pillow and tried not to remember the beating of wings and staring down on cities lit up like constellations and the Hunter repeating his warning.

Nos Galan Gaeaf, of course, he has no time for the living when he gathers the dead! The thought came to her between tears and sleeping and waking. As she drifted through bleariness she heard caterwauling and some part of her remembered how to slip the leash and take cat-form.

Sybil joined the circle of cats in William's barn; a tubby ginger, two scraggly tabbies, tortoiseshells, blacks with white feet and white snips, unaware of her own uncanny whiteness and blue eyes.

Together they slaked their sorrows until a farmlad climbed down a ladder with a knife: "If you lot don't shut up and disappear I swear I'll teach you!"

The other cats bounded away, but Sybil was delayed by the injury to her tendon. The blade fell, severing her left forepaw.

Sybil woke in agony with blood pouring from her severed wrist and soaking the bed. As she stared dumbly at her injury there was a knock on the door that roused William before it was opened by a servant with the farmlad carrying a white cat's paw and a wedding ring.

Sybil lost consciousness before she heard the exclamations of horror and accusations of witchcraft and did not awaken again.

The 'witch' of Bernshaw Tower was buried on unhallowed ground at Eagle's Crag. Some say her ghost is bound there and every Nos Galan Gaeaf she is doomed to relive her capture by William.

Those who have flown with wild swans tell her story differently. They say the Hunter answered Sybil's call and finally she met his hounds and saw his face and realised the white red-eared hound was the envious Mause Helton. She departed on her own wings and now flies with the Hunter over the lamp-lit cities he showed her centuries ago.

Last Breath

Our labour is lost.
Our bodies are ours no longer.
Our breath is torn from our lungs
to feed the might of Empire.

Our time is lost
to the clocks on the factory walls.
We shall forever be enslaved
until this Empire falls.

This Empire will not fall
until Annwn's doors are opened
and on the winds of our breath
the last words are spoken.

I am afraid these words, scrawled on a blood-stained
handkerchief, will be my last. Arthur's Empire has insinuated
itself into my lungs like the serpents of smoke wreathing from
the chimneys of the furnaces, blacking out the sun, strangling
the red brick streets.

I was born beneath its pall - the seventh of twelve children
tumbled top-to-tail in one bed. My parents put me to work
before I could read; sweeping beneath spinning engines,
piecing broken cotton, stuffing carding machines, until my
last job operating the looms.

My last job - I'm only twenty-five years old.

For years I have been coughing up cotton dust, lumps of coal, the blood of miners, chimney sweeps, piecers, spinners, weavers, watching it run down factory walls to join the poisoned river.

Unable to kill me from without Arthur's Empire is killing me from within, but I will not let it take my soul.

In this sanatorium grey people lie on white sheets, gasping in fevered air thick with sickness masked by wild indigo, permanganate of potash, white vitriol, carbolic acid, with which the stiff-uniformed nurses scrub the walls and floors as if they could erase illness, erase us. None of us have the breath to speak. We are simply waiting for the end.

Three nights ago Mr Humphries got out of bed and, leaning on his walking stick, pottered over to my bed, patted me on the shoulder and spoke in a husky voice, "There will be better worlds." The next morning I awoke staring at his corpse.

Some of the ghosts don't leave. I see them when I'm half-asleep, half-awake, drifting on laudanum. They mix with the ghosts of my past: Jonny the piecer with his leg crushed under a spinning engine; my mother, father, and sister Elsa coughing until their last gurgling breath; my wife... my poor wife Betty... dead in childbirth, with our child still inside her, screaming "Richard, help me!"

Betty was a breath of fresh air. When our eyes first met in the Moor Brook she was playing her flute and singing folksongs about the Old Grey Man, Will O Wisps, Peggy Lantern, the Lost Ones who followed gabbling hounds across the moors to a strange land and never returned.

She was a free spirit and I didn't want to bind her to my small life and long shifts operating looms in this mill town. Yet we were in love. She said she wanted to settle down, have a terrace of her own, babies to sing lullabies to, children to teach her songs to. She pretended not to mind working the spinning mules even though it drained her.

It was she who taught me to read and write (I was so embarrassed not knowing how). I had a talent for it, she said. Soon I was writing poetry, reciting it at the meetings of the Chartists on the moor. She told me I got carried away with campaigning for the ten percent, the votes for all working men, the constant struggles against the Cotton Lords.

She died during the Great Lock Out. I blamed myself. If we hadn't rebelled they wouldn't have locked us out of the factories and stopped our wages. With more to eat and less stress she'd have been stronger.

Now I see clearly it's the fault of this damned Empire that forced us to rebel. Still, it wracks me with grief that she never saw her first-born.

Betty joined the grey ghosts of those dead before their time in the maws of machines, shot down by police, riddled by the debilitating diseases that shift through the streets like smog. Sometimes I see her face, hear her playing a tune, trying to entice away the sorrowful crowds.

"They've forgotten the way back," the Gatherer of Souls explained the first time I saw him, dressed in funeral garments; a figure of calm amongst the distraught, reminding them of their names, introducing them to his hounds who entered like mist through the ventilation shafts and pushed damp noses into their hands.

"Back?" I croaked, an inexplicable longing filling my heart at his confirmation of an elsewhere. Some part of me rose up and followed as his hounds led the ghosts through cracks in the windows and he seated them on horses of night to ride with his barking pack through the skies.

I grasped hold of a black tail and was pulled away from the mills, the slums, the foul ditches, the smoking chimneys, across the moors to where the air was clean, then higher where the atmosphere grew thin.

We headed toward a star that was unendurably bright... or was that the light at the end of a dark tunnel? Its brightness was agonising. I lost my grip on the tail, fell back into this frail body, awoke with a jolt, gasping for breath, horse-hair corded between my fingers.

Where have they gone? Why can't I follow? Why must we die like this? I launched my thoughts like flying shuttles across the endless night.

Nothing but silence and the chink of hail on the window.

Tears squeezed from my eyes for the first time since I'd entered the sanatorium. I'd tried so hard not to feel sorry for myself or anybody else. Sobs threatened to choke me. I coughed up blood and fought not to wail as the voices of quintillions of ghosts answered, *you've forgotten*.

What have we forgotten?

Annwn. All the voices converged in the voice of a hailstone rattling against the window which took the appearance of a man's face with ice-rimmed cheekbones, commanding eyes, and a stern mouth.

A shiver of recognition ran through my fevered limbs. I hadn't heard that word in this life yet some part of me deep within remembered a moorland where clear streams flowed, golden plover flocked, and I might hear Betty playing her flute inside her grandmother's cottage and meet her grandmother and picnic with my ancestors.

An unseen hand offered me a white handkerchief to wipe my blood-stained lips.

I want to remember.

It's been a long forgetting.

Over the winter nights as I drifted like snow between waking and sleeping I was blown from Prydain across the seas to Affrica, India, America, Awstralia, to survey the extent of Empire.

As I witnessed battles between cotton lords and workers, slave traders and slaves, knights and infidels, I saw two dragons fighting breathlessly overhead with rent wings and ravaged lungs.

Both sides have forgotten and the Sleeping King dreams on.

I saw Arthur slamming the doors of Annwn shut then being laid to rest in a doorless cave, an endless river of blood flowing from his wound, a sword decorated with two intertwined serpents beside him.

Through a chink in a door I glimpsed giants; fearsome animals; human-like figures with the faces of birds wearing antlers or horns, hoofed, winged, dancing to instruments I couldn't name. Amongst them danced Betty with bare feet and whirling skirts calling me to join in.

I realised Arthur's Empire has sealed shut the doors to the world that contains our living past, our stories, our myths, the souls of innumerable others who do not look or think like us. *If we could regain that connection, break free, think what worlds we could create!*

When I came back to myself it was like surfacing from the deep. My lungs were on fire. Deeply embittered by knowing I would not be an opener of doors, I scrawled these final words, sadly doubting my handkerchief would be passed on to the Inspired Ones of the future. I wipe my lips for a final time and set it down on my bedside table.

I feel empty now. Empty of pain, empty of the detritus of Empire, empty of the urge to fight that drives the dragons to tear each other to pieces.

I hear the playing of a flute somewhere in the distance.

With my last breath I commend my soul to Annwn and feel myself released from Arthur's Empire.

The Gatherer of Souls pockets the blood-stained handkerchief I no longer need.

I am lifted through the brightness, inviting and wonderful, to where Betty is playing her flute, standing amidst cotton grass, enticing me to join her with a freckled smile, our child at her feet.

VI.
The Brink
of Time

The Oldest Animals 21st C

The Blackbirdsmith

stands at his anvil at the end of the world. His forge is his
yellow-rimmed burning eye, devouring all matter; it is the
Ring of Fire, the eclipse of our hot burnt-out sun, the
penumbra of a nuclear blast. His black feathered cloak was
sewn by the tailor who dressed the earth in cool rippling blues
and earthy browns. Each feather was stitched to his skin. His
sunlit beak is his hammer smashing down cruelly on the
shells of time, ripping out each aeon, wiping off the slime,
devouring the slippery squirming soft creatures. He takes a
worm in his tongs, hammers out the folds, sends it flying on
bat's wings as his final messenger. As he works he sings and
we all know that voice echoing from the edges so mellow and
sweet as he forges our dreams and black horses slide out of
the sea, *allan o'r mor*, to gallop through our nightmares.
There are furies in the hedgerows of our suburbs, apocalypses
swerving across our roads. There is a half-beat between death
and waking when hearts stand still.

The Wood Stag

carries the forest in his antlers. He was born with the
walking trees, winged souls singing in the velvety tines of his
branches amongst mosses, epiphytic ferns, squirrels running
faster than messages to keep time with what we call progress,

wrapping their tails round his mighty limbs. Every autumn the woodland swings as he rakes the ground, roaring hooves surrounded by musk-fog, clashes antlers, chases mates through the undergrowth of his russet mane. In winter they come with chainsaws to hack off his head, pin up the squirrels by their tails, leave the birds suspended in disbelief over the absence where forest was, nail his hollow skull with its grey and jagged tines and nostrils still pouring mist to a wall. In the empty lakes of his eyes he envisages spring, deer drinking at his waters, budding hawthorn. When he sprouts back to life, no hall, no prison of brick, can contain him.

The Wingless Owl

has a long history dating back to when her kind traversed this land on clawed feet amongst dinosaurs hooking up the earliest rodents, swallowing them whole, regurgitating the gunk of fur and bone: ancient debris, ancient fossils. After growing wings she enjoyed a bird's eye view of forest, plain, deep ocean wisdom, migrations of animals as the ice roved forward and melted back. Then in a blink of her eyes the landscape changed. Steeples appeared, walls between peoples, smoking heaps of brick that choked her and clattered out the silence of her wings. In an asphyxiation of shock her feathers fell out, floating down to cover the world in owly whiteness. Factories ceased steaming. Traffic stalled. From the high towers where one God rules, Arthur's knights looked up appalled by the red stumps of this wingless angel.

The Eagle Who Ate the Stars

nurses her burning tongue and the holes in her belly. She travelled to the end of the universe seeking answers, soaring on the thermals of the void, swooping, gliding her dihedral starship; breaking through the atmosphere, white tail blazing like a comet, before landing on a fist-sized stone. Nothing will close the black holes. The last remains of her pedestal are swallowed with her memories of feathered headdresses and bonnets, imperial flags, warplanes, astronomy, astrology, astrophysics. She learnt to explore the heights of space, but not to plummet the depths of Annwn, although she was taken down by a salmon, and in exchange removed the tridents, the nuclear warheads, from his spine. Is it any wonder they call her the eagle with the sunlit eye?

The Salmon of Wisdom

first-born egg, first-born alevin with his yolk-sac satchel, first-born fry with caudal and dorsal fins, first-born parr with red spots and camouflage stripes smolting and swimming downriver to the salty cold sea, returning with tail-thrust and salmon-leap to spill his nebula of milt. From a hazelnut he cracked the Awen and saw the waterways of time and space meet in his fish-eyes. He is afraid of fishers of knowledge. He has dwelled in this lake since fifty tridents were driven into his spine and the eagle performed her surgery leaving one hundred and fifty sutured salmon-pink scars. He wears armour now. His wisdom has become a submarine to sink beneath visions of witches, eyes on the radar, launch missiles at Mabon's prison, release the Sun-Child from the House of Stone: a deadly ray of light.

The Once and Future King has Returned

with his promises to make our country great again. He's reassembled his Knights of the Round Table with their hawkish eyes and pockets filled with pickings from the underworld.

He's won over the masses with charismatic bravado bragging about his dominion of an age when the nation was one.

He's going to build another wall to keep out the giants, clawing cats, dragons, dog-headed men, cast out all witches and eradicate all infidels from the world.

He's going to rebuild our military might. Prydwen is docked shining white as when she was hammered from the furnaces, surrounded by submarines, warheads glinting like his dyed blonde barnet.

His knights are mounting their metal-clad steeds, testing their wings, drip-feeding them oil and training their radar ears and swivel eyes.

He's amassing a stash of fiery swords and lightning lances. By the might of Caledfwlch he will regain control outside and in.

The capital is in the throes of disbelief. Shockwaves emanate from the Round Table. The financial centre is lit up, as if by the fire of the last sunset, but it's surrounded by darkness.

Whoever blew the horn and awakened the Once and Future King?

Fear is rising from damp patches beneath the armpits of a man in a pink shirt as he reads the evening news on the subway. It seeps up like miry fog to permeate the amygdalas of every brain.

The people are shee-shushing about the recension of health care and safe-guards for the greens and blues of the land to be trampled under hooves of metal horses dragging wagons from the pits of Annwn.

A witch's bracelets jangle. She smiles at an infidel. When they rub shoulders a small blister of hope bursts.

Who will call to the old gods denigrated by the Once and Future King whose God serves him?

To whom will you call?

Summer signed the pact long ago. He hides behind dark glasses as the sun grows warmer, seas lap at the land's toes, heels, ankles, as her corals shrink like flaccid plastics, her birds arrive at caterpillarless trees, her alpine flowers retreat to summits then wither and die.

When Winter defied him, his treasures were ripped from the underworld to fuel the ovens of floodlit palaces smothering the skies. He pays his tithe in jettisoning icebergs, walrus flippers, polar bear hides, confused geese. Winter will give the King's awakeners nothing. He says, "After all you have taken, what will you give me?"

Time

I.

I know you know of time in a way that defies the clocks.

I saw them stand still
in your untimely presence
and heard the silence of their unchiming,
the speechlessness of cuckoos hanging out on broken
 springs.

The falling cogs were glad to be released from their
 monotony.

I felt the clock within me breaking,
knew the senselessness of sixty seconds marked on a
 round face
measured by a rotating hand gloved like a clown's,
the ghastliest annoyance at ticking.

Timelines snapped like rulers bent too many times.

II.

I know of how you drank the Awen.

You showed me two serpents on your ring

biting down on their endings and clamping the secrets
of history into their mouths with their tails.

I did not understand until they became
red and white dragons with hooded necks
beside the deep well at the navel of Prydain
where the Awen bubbled like silver magma
and the whisperings of time grew louder:

"IT IS TIME IT IS TIME IT IS TIME."

You were conscious of what must be done
like an extended *déjà vu* echoing down a hall of mirrors.

When you burnt your tongue it felt like falling snowdrops.
Neither microscope nor telescope could compare
to your expanding and narrowing
of perception
nor the flight of a comet to your flight.

III.

I know that you broke free
and traversed time like a great white bird
imprinting every image on your retina
like the shadows of an
atom bomb,

taking the bit of dream between your teeth and bolting
outside our perception.

You watched the birthing of the universe,
the gathering of the earth,
her greening,
life erupting in tendril, tentacle, tail, and shell.

You hovered on the *jezt-zeit* of each mass extinction,
saw yourself gathering the souls

of stromatolites, trilobites, brachiopods, graptolites,
witnessing the burning temperatures
and rising sea levels,

earth as a glittering snowball
made of countless frozen souls.

When you saw the approaching meteor
you fled into the warren
of a soft marsupial,
clamped
your hands over your ears as the earth rocked,

saw yourself hauling the souls of smoking dinosaurs
back into the core of the earth's soul
and giving them a place
in myth.

You saw yourself standing in my now
filled with the smouldering souls of dead warriors,
poets, rebels, madmen, dreamers, clamouring for change
as the sea levels rose again with new islands
of plastic where birds left their fallen,
flowers withered and insects fell
through your fingers
like sand

as you fought to stand the hourglass up again,
kick into reverse the mighty engine of the Anthropocene.

The last thing you saw was a city of butterflies
gathered from the mouths
of the dead.

IV.

I know you locked your visions behind darkened glass,
in the riddles of your speechless dead
and stone-tongued bards.

Some say the language of dragons left you tongue-tied,
yet I heard you singing our soul-names,
calling us back

as the glass shatters and the dragons roar and the Awen
bursts from the well,

to stand with you on the brink of time.

Witches of Annwn

'Arthur said, "Are there any of the wonders we have still not obtained?"

One of the men said, "Yes, the blood of the Very Black Witch, daughter of the Very White Witch from Pennant Gofid in the uplands of hell."

Arthur set out for the North'
Culhwch and Olwen

I take the phial containing the last drop of Orddu's blood from my refrigerator.

Last night I broke the bottles into which Arthur drained her life's essence fifteen hundred years ago.

The breaking of Gwyddolwyn's bottles was no less difficult than shattering a history dominated by Arthurian warlords in which witches, women, people with black skin, and those associated with black magic and Annwn's shadowy fecund depths have persistently been persecuted.

As I hefted the dwarven hammer and invoked the fury of Gwyn ap Nudd and the spirits of Annwn and the bottles shattered into a million rainbow shards I felt countless souls released from the glass edifices of Arthur's Empire.

The blood splattering the walls of my cellar reminded me of how it had been shed. Howling into my ears came the voices of all Arthur's victims from the first Dark Age to this one. As I scooped up that tiny bead, that miniscule drop, it came to represent her and every one of them.

Tonight it will be returned to Pennant Gofid.

It's Nos Galan Gaeaf. The wind is getting up. Whistling ghosts are rattling plates and glasses beside my sink. Rain sluices my window. Beyond the terraces the swollen Ribble runs grey through the park. It's said the Samlesbury witches danced with black dogs upriver at Red Scar.

There's no possibility of seeing mysterious whale-like Pendle adrift in its sea of mist through this downpour. I think of the Pendle Witch pub, Witch's Brew Ale, images of witches on broomsticks masking traumatised ghosts who have forgotten how to brew or fly.

Arthur will soon be reviving the witch hunts. This drop of blood is our only chance.

I turn to my altar. The cloth is black to reflect the season. In the centre stands a statue of Gwyn ap Nudd, bull-horned, spear in hand, with a white red-nosed hound beside him. Incense swirls around him like mist. The Very Black candle I lit for Orddu has almost burned down.

"I seek your blessing in all I do tonight." My heart is pounding and my palms are damp.

Gwyn's statue glows with an otherworldly light. I glimpse a portal opening behind him, stars spiralling, hear the Song of the Universe. Its beauty fills my heart with the promise of another world.

"Thank you."

In the absence where the Very Black candle stood, Orddu appears, a tall candle-like shadow.

"I know you will be with me."

Outside it's raining cats and dogs. I wouldn't be surprised to see red-eyed rats swimming up from the sewers. Candlelit pumpkins lurk with tombstone grins. Hordes of trick-or-treaters wearing witch's masks or bed-sheets with runny felt-tip faces blow by on Annwn's winds.

In the city centre armoured knights patrol on metal-clad horses, visors down, lances dripping in the rain. A giant limps down the main street, dragging his bloody beard, leaving a glistening Cherryade-like trail. Packs of dog-heads fight with cat-heads. Nine headless witches carry their cloven heads, handing out mouthfuls of brains.

A passing bell sounds and the crowd parts for a procession of homeless people in red caps and ragged funeral garments, chanting mournfully, bearing Arthur's corpse on a blood-stained bier.

The bars are full of zombies and murder victims necking pints with eyeballs in the bottom, Bloody Marys, shots of ectoplasmic goo. A girl walks by with a trolley of radioactive test-tubes. I close my hand on the phial: there are knights dressed as vampires hungry for witch's blood.

On the bus station a guitarist wearing a stick-on red beard is singing Arthur's death-song. I walk past the bus stands to number 81 where Morgan's chariot awaits pulled by two black shaggy-fetlocked horses.

"To Pennant Gofid." I pay my fee to the driver with the flat cap and scarred cheek.

A moment later I step out in the northern uplands. Few feet have walked these paths that lead from the land into myth, from Thisworld into Annwn, into the liminal spaces where magic is done.

As the rain abates and the waxing moon breaks through the clouds a crow caws her welcome. I look down into the steep valley where the White River roars flanked by barren trees and a fog of ghosts. In the northern cliff face is the cave where Orddu was born and met her end.

Following a precipitous path skirting the vale I think of Snow's arrival and all who journeyed here to seek advice. I recall my last journey and the Very Great Grandmother's little finger on the index of a history book referring me to its last page.

A skull on the wayside and a gaping ribcage remind me of those who didn't make it. Too many came without respect: dozens of knights frozen dead by the gazes of the men-in-the-boulders, others who threw themselves down precipices maddened by howling ghost-wolves.

Of course, one party was successful, and I can't help thinking about them: Arthur with Gwythyr, his knights, three servants, Caw with the bottles and Hygwydd carrying the cauldron that boiled Orddu's bones.

The thought chills me more than the wolf songs and mournful cries echoing from the cliffs. My hands are numb and Orddu's blood is growing cold. Yet a warm orange glow emanates from the cave and the silhouette of a stout old woman beckons me on. Don't look back...

The Very Great Grandmother greets me with a bowl of stew from her animal-skin cauldron. Her descendants are gathered in reindeer hides, wolf furs, and woollen cloaks with rattling tooth-and-bone jewellery. Some lean on staffs or ancient weapons. Orddu cannot be seen, but her presence grows as I warm my hands and the phial at the flames.

Once I have regained my strength I step to the entrance and stand beside the White Spring. Misty shades of warriors rise from the White River to surround me. The crow watches with an expectorant black eye from an overhanging branch.

In the distance I hear hoofbeats and a dull clank-clank. My heart jolts with lightning-like terror. Hastily I unstopper the phial and speak, "For thousands of years Inspired Ones, witches, have been guardians of this valley. Fifteen hundred years ago Arthur slaughtered Orddu, 'Very Black', the Last Witch of Pennant Gofid. By draining her blood he stole the power of magical women.

"The bottles have been broken. Tonight I return the last drop of Orddu's blood to where her bones are buried so she can be whole. To complete the river of blood flowing back to Orwen..." I speak the names "to Wind Singer... to Snow... to her Very Great Grandmother. To free all witches, all women, all souls from Arthur's thrall."

Crouching, I pour the blood into the earth. As it glistens in the moonlight I am aware of the moon's sombre stare and the stilling of the stars in a perfect pattern reflected in its surface. Then with their silvery reflection it seeps away, leaving a crimson stain on the cold soil.

The crow carps her delight as Orddu appears black-cloaked, black hair braided, black eyes once hard as jet filled with joy and relief as she embraces her ancestors in turn. She turns to me, "Thank you for releasing me." Her voice is hoarse and whispery with misuse like a corvid's.

"Tonight Arthur and his Empire will fall," Orddu states with quiet triumph. "Like I did, you must stand firm and trust in our vision: a gift of the Awen, from Annwn, from Gwyn ap Nudd."

As the hoofbeats louden and the clanking rises to sound like the bell of a cursed ship I see the procession approaching on the pathway. Arthur is aboard a gigantic dappled mare with a heavy head and lumbering gait, serpent-sword slung across his back, knife-hilt glimmering. Gwythyr on a golden stallion and two armoured knights on metal-clad warhorses accompany him. Three servants struggle with heavy packs. Hygwydd staggers under the weight of the cauldron. Caw brings new bottles stamped by another dwarven hand.

"Stand firm," says Orddu, "and the magic Arthur worked fifteen hundred years ago will be reversed."

Then she and her ancestors are gone. The fire goes out leaving the cave dark and empty. Like her I stand alone. My only weapons are my bare hands and I'm no fighter. Yet I've foreseen the end in the starry pattern in the Last Witch of Pennant Gofid's last drop of blood.

Arthur draws Llamrei to a halt. His cold blue eyes are lifeless as the North Star. His square-jawed face is pale beneath his helm, his lips whiter, reminding me of his corpse on the blood-stained bier.

"I detect the doing of black magic," Arthur speaks in a voice hollow as the hills from which he returned, "the raising of black ghosts. I see evil has returned to Pennant Gofid in the form of a woman."

Summoning my courage I retort, "The only evil that has ever entered this valley is you and your knights. Your religion created evil."

"Heresy," Arthur growls. "The price for witchcraft is death."

"You're too late," I taunt him. "Orddu's blood has been returned. The magic by which you prolonged your lives and kept us servile is at an end. Can't you see that, like your Empire, you are dying?"

Arthur's jaw trembles.

The cauldron rolls off Hygwydd's shoulders as he falls to his knees. His face is badly burnt, his eyes stare from hollow sockets. He puts a patchy, blistered hand to his cheek and it falls away.

Arthur stares at Hygwydd in horror. "But..."

"You were never master of the cauldron or the mysteries of life and death. Your refusal to die has been one long lie."

Arthur's hand goes reflexively to his side.

"All the herbs of Morgana and the pharmaceuticals of modern medicine never healed your wound."

Blood begins to trickle from beneath Arthur's mail.

"No," Arthur shakes his head in denial. "I am the Once and Future King. Whilst I can kill I still live!" He draws Caledfwlch and the serpents hiss into life breathing jets of flame.

Stand firm. I hold onto Orddu's words as the heat sears my skin. Recalling her death I see my approaching death reflected in the golden eyes of the serpents. *If that's what it takes.* "Kill me. Kill one more woman. Kill one more witch. We'll be waiting for you in Annwn."

Face twisted into a demonic mask by fathomless hatred, Arthur swings his sword.

A blood-curdling howl resonates around the valley.

Arthur looks up at the huge white wolf staring down from the Howling Rocks. The knees of his mare and the horses of his knights buckle. Thrown forward, he sprawls belly-first from his saddle, dropping his sword. Its fire goes out and the serpents slither into the undergrowth.

Forcing himself groggily to his knees, Arthur reaches for Carwennan, the knife that killed Orddu, lips peeled back from his teeth in a hateful grimace. Blood pours from his wound down his thigh and pools around him as his trembling hand closes on the white hilt.

Too weak to draw his knife, he sways in horror as the wolf pounces down from the Howling Rocks and bounds toward him, getting smaller the closer it gets, shifting into a white red-eared hound.

When it sniffs at his blood Arthur opens his mouth to scream, but nothing comes out. He gags on the gazes of his victims reflected in the hound's eyes as his life flows out and is lapped up by the eager tongue.

Savagely the hound tears off Arthur's armour, rips out his soul, and grips it in strong jaws as it growls and struggles as a gristled old cave bear, a wyrm, a fiery bird, a clew of worms, a scorpion, a sharp-tusked boar, a squealing piglet... until it becomes a whimpering bear-cub.

The hound carries Arthur's soul by the scruff of the neck into the cave, followed by his pack bearing the souls of the knights and servants.

Gwythyr is the only man who remains mounted. He puts his spurs to the sides of his golden stallion and departs at a break-neck gallop. They vanish with a scream of rocks as the moon announces midnight.

The triumphant blast of a horn sounds overhead as the Hunter in the Skies amasses his pack; toothed, hoofed, horned, furred, feathered, clawed, winged. As one fierce unstoppable beast they ride to gather the ruins of Arthur's Empire and clear the way for the next world.

I light a fire beneath the cauldron to rekindle our magic and celebrate with Orddu and the witches of Annwn until the sun rises to fill our sacred valley with a new dawn.

Acknowledgements

With special thanks to my mum and dad for providing me with a room and food, which has made it possible for me to give my full attention to writing this book. A big thank you to Peter Dillon for commenting on and proofreading the manuscript. I'm very grateful to Greg Hill for his new translation of 'The Conversation Between Gwyn ap Nudd and Gwyddno Garanhir' and help and advice on Welsh mythology and language. Thanks to Gods & Radicals for publishing and supporting my work and to the Oak and Feather Grove, Way of the Buzzard drumming circle, and Damson Poets for friendship and support on my journey. Many thanks to Rhyd Wildermuth and Gods & Radicals Press for publishing my books, firstly in digital form, and now in print, and for helping me to reach a wider audience.

Finally I would like to thank all my patrons, whose financial support has been invaluable, in particular:
Greg Hill
Rachel O'Meara

'Myrddin's Scribe' and 'After Procopius' were previously published in *A Beautiful Resistance* 2 and 3 and 'Hunter in the Skies' in *Pagan Dawn*.

Lorna Smithers

Lorna is a poet, author, awenydd, Brythonic polytheist, and devotee of Gwyn ap Nudd. Her three books: *Enchanting the Shadowlands*, *The Broken Cauldron*, and *Gatherer of Souls* are published by the Ritona imprint of Gods & Radicals Press. Based in Penwortham, Lancashire, North West England, she is a conservation intern and allotmenteer who is learning to grow small green things and listen to the land. She blogs at 'From Peneverdant.'

Printed in the USA
CPSIA information can be obtained
at www.ICGtesting.com
JSHW010023171123
51894JS00011B/165